Poems of the American Spirit

Poems of the American Spirit

Series Editor
David Stanford Burr

Barnes & Noble Poetry Library

The acknowledgments appearing on page 233
constitute an extension of this copyright page.

2002 Barnes & Noble Books

ISBN 0-7607-3312-0

Text design by Rhea Braunstein

Printed and bound in the United States of America

02 03 04 05 M 9 8 7 6 5 4 3 2 1

RRD-C

Contents

Foreword

America fought a war of independence from Britain, created a democratic republic based on an inspired constitution, endured a bloody civil war, and sent out its bright beacon of promise to people "yearning to breathe free." In this compelling anthology, *Poems of the American Spirit,* some of our greatest poets—Walt Whitman, Emily Dickinson, Robert Frost, and Carl Sandburg—celebrate our nation's unique history and rich heritage of liberty and justice.

The exploits of our pantheon of national heroes—familiar names such as Paul Revere, Betsy Ross, Nathan Hale, Molly Pitcher, George Washington, Thomas Jefferson, John Adams, John Hancock, Patrick Henry, Daniel Boone, Jim Bowie, Davy Crockett, John Brown, Barbara Frietchie, Robert E. Lee, Abraham Lincoln—are enshrined in the poems of thankful poets and proud Americans. Patriot Thomas Paine calls for the defense of our "Liberty Tree" from England's tyranny; John Quincy Adams, our sixth president, passionately exalts justice; and First Lady Dolley Madison gives grateful thanks to the Marquis de Lafayette for his help in our struggle for independence. Slaves sing the "Drinking Gourd" song so they might follow the Big Dipper's stars to freedom; freed slaves sing the "Civil War Chant" as they march off to secure the Union and their liberty; and Langston Hughes and Maya Angelou sing of dreams and hope for all American peoples, races, and creeds.

In these poems, the "land of the free" rings out "from sea to shining sea," from the "home on the range" to the cities—Philadelphia, New York, Boston, Chicago. They commemorate the Liberty Bell, the Statue of Liberty, the Congressional Library, that brave folk hero and engineer Casey Jones—even the nation's pastime and Mudville's mighty Casey.

Poems of the American Spirit is an opportunity to refresh our memories of classic American paeans we may not have read for a while: "Listen, my children, and you shall hear." It is a reminder of what we as a people and a nation are about and of what America the beautiful is—our land, our home, sweet home.

—DAVID STANFORD BURR

Poems of the American Spirit

The Gift Outright

The land was ours before we were the land's.
She was our land more than a hundred years
Before we were her people. She was ours
In Massachusetts, in Virginia,
But we were England's, still colonials,
Possessing what we still were unpossessed by,
Possessed by what we now no more possessed.
Something we were withholding made us weak
Until we found it was ourselves
We were withholding from our land of living,
And forthwith found salvation in surrender.
Such as we were we gave ourselves outright
(The deed of gift was many deeds of war)
To the land vaguely realizing westward,
But still unstoried, artless, unenhanced,
Such as she was, such as she would become.

ROBERT FROST (1874–1963)

Columbus

Behind him lay the gray Azores,
  Behind the Gates of Hercules;
Before him not the ghost of shores,
  Before him only shoreless seas.
The good mate said: "Now must we pray,
  For lo! the very stars are gone.
Brave Admiral, speak, what shall I say?"
  "Why, say 'Sail on! sail on! and on!' "

"My men grow mutinous day by day;
  My men grow ghastly wan and weak."
The stout mate thought of home; a spray
  Of salt wave washed his swarthy cheek.
"What shall I say, brave Admiral, say,
  If we sight naught but seas at dawn?"
"Why, you shall say at break of day,
  'Sail on! sail on! sail on! and on!' "

They sailed and sailed, as winds might blow,
  Until at last the blanched mate said:
"Why, now not even God would know
  Should I and all my men fall dead.
These very winds forget their way,
  For God from these dread seas is gone.
Now speak, brave Admiral, speak and say"—
  He said: "Sail on! sail on! and on!"

JOAQUIN MILLER (1841–1913)

They sailed. They sailed. Then spake the mate:
  "This mad sea shows his teeth to-night.
He curls his lip, he lies in wait,
  With lifted teeth, as if to bite!
Brave Admiral, say but one good word:
  What shall we do when hope is gone?"
The words leapt like a leaping sword:
  "Sail on! sail on! sail on! and on!"

Then, pale and worn, he kept his deck,
  And peered through darkness. Ah, that night
Of all dark nights! And then a speck—
  A light! a light! a light! a light!
It grew, a starlit flag unfurled!
  It grew to be Time's burst of dawn.
He gained a world; he gave that world
  Its grandest lesson: "On! sail on!"

The Landing of the Pilgrim Fathers

The breaking waves dashed high
  On a stern and rock-bound coast,
And the woods, against a stormy sky,
  Their giant branches tossed;

And the heavy night hung dark
  The hills and waters o'er,
When a band of exiles moored their bark
  On the wild New England shore.

Not as the conqueror comes,
  They, the true-hearted, came:
Not with the roll of the stirring drums,
  And the trumpet that sings of fame;

Not as the flying come,
  In silence and in fear,—
They shook the depths of the desert's gloom
  With their hymns of lofty cheer.

Amidst the storm they sang,
  And the stars heard, and the sea;
And the sounding aisles of the dim woods rang
  To the anthem of the free!

FELICIA DOROTHEA HEMANS (1793–1835)

The ocean-eagle soared
  From his nest by the white wave's foam,
And the rocking pines of the forest roared;
  This was their welcome home!

There were men with hoary hair
  Amidst that pilgrim-band;
Why had they come to wither there,
  Away from their childhood's land?

There was woman's fearless eye,
  Lit by her deep love's truth;
There was manhood's brow, serenely high,
  And the fiery heart of youth.

What sought they thus afar?
  Bright jewels of the mine?
The wealth of seas, the spoils of war?—
  They sought a faith's pure shrine!

Aye, call it holy ground,
  The soil where first they trod!
They have left unstained what there they found—
  Freedom to worship God!

FELICIA DOROTHEA HEMANS (1793–1835)

The Mayflower

Down in the bleak December bay
The ghostly vessel stands away;
Her spars and halyards white with ice,
Under the dark December skies.
A hundred souls, in company,
Have left the vessel pensively,—
Have reached the frosty desert there,
And touched it with the knees of prayer.
  And now the day begins to dip,
The night begins to lower
  Over the bay, and over the ship
    Mayflower.

Neither the desert nor the sea
Imposes rites: their prayers are free;
Danger and toil the wild imposes,
And thorns must grow before the roses.
And who are these?—and what distress
The savage-acred wilderness
On mother, maid, and child may bring,
Beseems them for a fearful thing;
  For now the day begins to dip,
The night begins to lower
  Over the bay, and over the ship
    Mayflower.

But Carver leads (in heart and health
A hero of the commonwealth)
The axes that the camp requires,
To build the lodge, and heap the fires.
And Standish from his warlike store
Arrays his men along the shore,
Distributes weapons resonant,
And dons his harness militant;
  For now the day begins to dip,
The night begins to lower
  Over the bay, and over the ship
    Mayflower;

And Rose, his wife, unlocks a chest—
She sees a Book, in vellum dressed,
She drops a tear, and kisses the tome,
Thinking of England and of home:
Might they—the Pilgrims, there and then
Ordained to do the work of men—
Have seen, in visions of the air,
While pillowed on the breast of prayer
  (When now the day began to dip,
The night began to lower
  Over the bay, and over the ship
    Mayflower),

continues

The Canaan of their wilderness
A boundless empire of success;
And seen the years of future nights
Jewelled with myriad household lights;
And seen the honey fill the hive;
And seen a thousand ships arrive;
And heard the wheels of travel go;
It would have cheered a thought of woe,
  When now the day began to dip,
The night began to lower
  Over the bay, and over the ship
    Mayflower.

The Pilgrim Fathers

The Pilgrim Fathers, —where are they?
  The waves that brought them o'er
Still roll in the bay, and throw their spray
  As they break along the shore;
Still roll in the bay, as they rolled that day
  When the Mayflower moored below;
When the sea around was black with storms,
  And white the shore with snow.

The mists that wrapped the Pilgrim's sleep
  Still brood upon the tide;
And his rocks yet keep their watch by the deep
  To stay its waves of pride.
But the snow-white sail that he gave to the gale,
  When the heavens looked dark, is gone,—
As an angel's wing through an opening cloud
  Is seen, and then withdrawn.

The pilgrim exile, —sainted name!
  The hill whose icy brow
Rejoiced, when he came, in the morning's flame,
  In the morning's flame burns now.
And the moon's cold light, as it lay that night
  On the hillside and the sea,

stanza continues

Still lies where he laid his houseless head,—
But the Pilgrim,—where is he?

The Pilgrim Fathers are at rest:
When summer's throned on high,
And the world's warm breast is in verdure dressed,
Go, stand on the hill where they lie.
The earliest ray of the golden day
On that hallowed spot is cast;
And the evening sun, as he leaves the world,
Looks kindly on that spot last.

The Pilgrim spirit has not fled:
It walks in noon's broad light;
And it watches the bed of the glorious dead,
With the holy stars, by night.
It watches the bed of the brave who have bled,
And still guard this ice-bound shore,
Till the waves of the bay, where the Mayflower lay,
Shall foam and freeze no more.

The First Thanksgiving Day

In Puritan New England a year had passed away
Since first beside the Plymouth coast the English
Mayflower lay,
When Bradford, the good Governor, sent fowlers
forth to snare
The turkey and the wild-fowl, to increase the
scanty fare:—

"Our husbandry hath prospered, there is corn
enough for food,
Though the peas be parched in blossom, and the
grain indifferent good.
Who blessed the loaves and fishes for the feast
miraculous,
And filled the widow's cruse, He hath remembered us!

"Give thanks unto the Lord of Hosts, by whom we
all are fed,
Who granted us our daily prayer, 'Give us our
daily bread!'
By us and by our children let this day be kept
for aye,
In memory of His bounty, as the land's
Thanksgiving Day."

continues

ALICE WILLIAMS BROTHERTON (19TH CENTURY)

Each brought his share of Indian meal the pious
feast to make,
With the fat deer from the forest and the wild fowl
from the brake.
And chanted hymn and prayer were raised—
though eyes with tears were dim—
"The Lord He hath remembered us, let us
remember Him!"

Then Bradford stood up at their head and lifted up
his voice:
"The corn is gathered from the field, I call you
to rejoice;
Thank God for all His mercies, from the greatest
to the least,
Together we have *fasted,* friends, together let us *feast.*

"The Lord who led forth Israel was with us in
the waste:
Sometime in light, sometime in cloud, before us He
hath paced;
Now give Him thanks, and pray to Him who holds
us in His hand
To prosper us and make of this a strong and
mighty land!"

From Plymouth to the Golden Gate to-day their
children tread,
The mercies of that bounteous Hand upon the land
are shed;
The "flocks are on a thousand hill," the prairies
wave with grain,
The cities spring like mushrooms now where once
was desert-plain.

Heap high the board with plenteous cheer and
gather to the feast,
And toast that sturdy Pilgrim band whose courage
never ceased.
Give praise to that All Gracious One by whom
their steps were led,
And thanks unto the harvest's Lord who sends our
"daily bread."

ALICE WILLIAMS BROTHERTON (19TH CENTURY)

from The Brother Indian

Boast not, proud English, of thy birth and blood:
Thy Brother Indian is by birth as good.
Of one blood God made Him, and Thee, and All—
As wise, as faire, as strong, as personall.
By nature, wrath's his portion, thine, no more
Till Grace his soule and thine in Christ restore.
Make sure thy second birth, else thou shalt see
Heaven ope to Indians wild, but shut to thee.

The Indian Burying Ground

In spite of all the learned have said,
I still my old opinion keep;
The *posture,* that *we* give the dead,
Points out the soul's eternal sleep.

Not so the ancients of these lands—
The Indian, when from life released,
Again is seated with his friends,
And shares again the joyous feast.

His imaged birds, and painted bowl,
And venison, for a journey dressed,
Bespeak the nature of the soul,
ACTIVITY, that knows no rest.

His bow, for action ready bent,
And arrows, with a head of stone,
Can only mean that life is spent,
And not the old ideas gone.

Thou, stranger, that shalt come this way,
No fraud upon the dead commit—
Observe the swelling turf, and say
They do not *lie,* but here they *sit.*

continues

PHILIP FRENEAU (1752–1832)

Here still a lofty rock remains,
On which the curious eye may trace
(Now wasted, half, by wearing rains)
The fancies of a ruder race.

Here still an aged elm aspires,
Beneath whose far-projecting shade
(And which the shepherd still admires)
The children of the forest played!

There oft a restless Indian queen
(Pale *Shebah,* with her braided hair)
And many a barbarous form is seen
To chide the man that lingers there.

By midnight moons, o'er moistening dews,
In habit for the chase arrayed,
The hunter still the deer pursues,
The hunter and the deer, a shade!

And long shall timorous fancy see
The painted chief, and pointed spear,
And Reason's self shall bow the knee
To shadows and delusions here.

Hiawatha's Childhood

from *THE SONG OF HIAWATHA*

By the shores of Gitche Gumee,
By the shining Big-Sea-Water,
Stood the wigwam of Nokomis,
Daughter of the Moon, Nokomis.
Dark behind it rose the forest,
Rose the black and gloomy pine-trees,
Rose the firs with cones upon them;
Bright before it beat the water,
Beat the clear and sunny water,
Beat the shining Big-Sea-Water.
  There the wrinkled old Nokomis
Nursed the little Hiawatha,
Rocked him in his linden cradle,
Bedded soft in moss and rushes,
Safely bound with reindeer sinews;
Stilled his fretful wail by saying,
"Hush! the Naked bear will hear thee!"
Lulled him into slumber, singing,
"Ewa-yea! my little owlet!
Who is this, that lights the wigwam?
With his great eyes lights the wigwam?
Ewa-yea! my little owlet!"

continues

HENRY WADSWORTH LONGFELLOW (1807–1882)

Many things Nokomis taught him
Of the stars that shine in heaven;
Showed him Ishkoodah, the comet,
Ishkoodah, with fiery tresses;
Showed the Death-Dance of the spirits,
Warriors with their plumes and war-clubs,
Flaring far away to northward
In the frosty nights of winter;
Showed the broad white road in heaven,
Pathway of the ghosts, the shadows,
Running straight across the heavens,
Crowded with the ghosts, the shadows.

At the door on summer evenings,
Sat the little Hiawatha;
Heard the whispering of the pine-trees,
Heard the lapping of the waters,
Sounds of music, words of wonder;
"Minne-wawa!" said the pine-trees.
"Mudway-aushka!" said the water.

Saw the fire-fly Wah-wah-taysee,
Flitting through the dusk of evening,
With the twinkle of its candle
Lighting up the brakes and bushes,
And he sang the song of children,
Sang the song Nokomis taught him:
"Wah-wah-taysee, little fire-fly,
Little, flitting, white-fire insect,
Little, dancing, white-fire creature,

Light me with your little candle,
Ere upon my bed I lay me,
Ere in sleep I close my eyelids!"
  Saw the moon rise from the water,
Rippling, rounding from the water,
Saw the flecks and shadows on it,
Whispered, "What is that, Nokomis?"
And the good Nokomis answered:
"Once a warrior, very angry,
Seized his grandmother, and threw her
Up into the sky at midnight;
Right against the moon he threw her;
'Tis her body that you see there."
  Saw the rainbow in the heaven,
In the eastern sky the rainbow,
Whispered, "What is that, Nokomis?"
And the good Nokomis answered:
" 'Tis the heaven of flowers you see there;
All the wild-flowers of the forest,
All the lilies of the prairie,
When on earth they fade and perish,
Blossom in that heaven above us."
  When he heard the owls at midnight,
Hooting, laughing in the forest,
"What is that?" he cried in terror;
"What is that," he said, "Nokomis?"

continues

And the good Nokomis answered:
"That is but the owl and owlet,
Talking in their native language,
Talking, scolding at each other."
  Then the little Hiawatha
Learned of every bird its language,
Learned their names and all their secrets,
How they built their nests in summer,
Where they hid themselves in winter,
Talked with them whene'er he met them,
Called them "Hiawatha's Chickens."
  Of all beasts he learned the language,
Learned their names and all their secrets,
How the beavers built their lodges,
Where the squirrels hid their acorns,
How the reindeer ran so swiftly,
Why the rabbit was so timid,
Talked with them whene'er he met them,
Called them "Hiawatha's Brothers."

Home, Sweet Home!

'Mid pleasures and palaces though we may roam,
Be it ever so humble, there's *no* place like home.
A charm from the sky seems to hallow us there,
Which, seek through the *world,* is ne'er met with
elsewhere.
Home! sweet home!
There's no place like home!

An exile from home, splendour dazzles in vain!
Oh! give me my lowly thatch'd cottage again!
The birds singing gaily that came at my call,
Give me *them,* with the *peace of mind* DEARER
than all!
Home! sweet home!
There's no place like home!

JOHN HOWARD PAYNE (1791–1852)

The Village Blacksmith

Under a spreading chestnut-tree
  The village smithy stands;
The smith, a mighty man is he,
  With large and sinewy hands;
And the muscles of his brawny arms
  Are strong as iron bands.

His hair is crisp, and black, and long,
  His face is like the tan;
His brow is wet with honest sweat,
  He earns whate'er he can,
And looks the whole world in the face,
  For he owes not any man.

Week in, week out, from morn till night,
  You can hear his bellows blow;
You can hear him swing his heavy sledge
  With measured beat and slow,
Like a sexton ringing the village bell,
  When the evening sun is low.

And children coming home from school
  Look in at the open door;
They love to see the flaming forge,

stanza continues

And hear the bellows roar,
And catch the burning sparks that fly
Like chaff from a threshing-floor.

He goes on Sunday to the church,
And sits among his boys;
He hears the parson pray and preach,
He hears his daughter's voice,
Singing in the village choir,
And it makes his heart rejoice.

It sounds to him like her mother's voice,
Singing in Paradise!
He needs must think of her once more,
How in the grave she lies;
And with his hard, rough hand he wipes
A tear out of his eyes.

Toiling, —rejoicing, —sorrowing,
Onward through life he goes;
Each morning sees some task begin,
Each evening sees it close;
Something attempted, something done,
Has earned a night's repose.

continues

Thanks, thanks to thee, my worthy friend,
  For the lesson thou hast taught!
Thus at the flaming forge of life
  Our fortunes must be wrought;
Thus on its sounding anvil shaped
  Each burning deed and thought!

Liberty Tree

In a chariot of light from the regions of day,
  The Goddess of Liberty came;
Ten thousand celestials directed the way,
  And hither conducted the dame.
A fair budding branch from the gardens above,
  Where millions with millions agree,
She brought in her hand as a pledge of her love,
  And the plant she named Liberty Tree.

The celestial exotic struck deep in the ground,
  Like a native it flourished and bore;
The fame of its fruit drew the nations around,
  To seek out this peaceable shore.
Unmindful of names or distinction they came,
  For freemen like brothers agree;
With one spirit endued, they one friendship
    pursued,
  And their temple was Liberty Tree.

Beneath this fair tree, like the patriarchs of old,
  Their bread in contentment they ate,
Unvexed with the troubles of silver and gold,
  The cares of the grand and the great.

stanza continues

With timber and tar they Old England supplied,
And supported her power on the sea;
Her battles they fought, without getting a groat,
For the honor of Liberty Tree.

But hear, O ye swains, 'tis a tale most profane,
How all the tyrannical powers,
Kings, Commons, and Lords, are united amain,
To cut down this guardian of ours;
From the east to the west blow the trumpet to
arms,
Through the land let the sound of it flee,
Let the far and the near, all unite with a cheer,
In defence of our Liberty Tree.

A Ballad of the Boston Tea-Party

No! never such a draught was poured
Since Hebe served with nectar
The bright Olympians and their Lord,
Her over-kind protector, —

Since Father Noah squeezed the grape
And took to such behaving
As would have shamed our grandsire ape
Before the days of shaving, —

No! ne'er was mingled such a draught
In palace, hall, or arbor,
As freemen brewed and tyrants quaffed
That night in Boston Harbor!

It kept King George so long awake
His brain at last got addled,
It made the nerves of Britain shake,
With sevenscore millions saddled;

Before that bitter cup was drained
Amid the roar of cannon,
The Western war-cloud's crimson stained
The Thames, the Clyde, the Shannon;

continues

OLIVER WENDELL HOLMES (1809–1894)

Full many a six-foot grenadier
The flattened grass had measured,
And many a mother many a year
Her tearful memories treasured;

Fast spread the tempest's darkening pall,
The mighty realms were troubled,
The storm broke loose, but first of all
The Boston teapot bubbled!

An evening party, — only that,
No formal invitation,
No gold-laced coat, no stiff cravat,
No feast in contemplation,

No silk-robed dames, no fiddling band,
No flowers, no songs, no dancing, —
A tribe of red men, axe in hand, —
Behold the guests advancing!

How fast the stragglers join the throng,
From stall and workshop gathered!
The lively barber skips along
And leaves a chin half-lathered;

The smith has flung his hammer down,—
The horseshoe still is glowing;
The truant tapster at the Crown
Has left a beer-cask flowing;

The cooper's boys have dropped the adze,
And trot behind their master;
Up run the tarry ship-yard lads,—
The crowd is hurrying faster,—

Out from the Millpond's purlieus gush
The streams of white-faced millers,
And down their slippery alleys rush
The lusty young Fort-Hillers;

The ropewalk lends its 'prentice crew,—
The tories seize the omen:
"Ay, boys, you'll soon have work to do
For England's rebel foemen,

'King Hancock,' Adams, and their gang,
That fire the mob with treason,—
When these we shoot and those we hang
The town will come to reason."

continues

On — on to where the tea-ships ride!
And now their ranks are forming, —
A rush, and up the *Dartmouth*'s side
The Mohawk band is swarming!

See the fierce natives! What a glimpse
Of paint and fur and feather,
As all at once the full-grown imps
Light on the deck together!

A scarf the pigtail's secret keeps,
A blanket hides the breeches, —
And out the cursèd cargo leaps,
And overboard it pitches!

O woman, at the evening board
So gracious, sweet, and purring,
So happy while the tea is poured,
So blest while spoons are stirring,

What martyr can compare with thee,
The mother, wife, or daughter,
That night, instead of best Bohea,
Condemned to milk and water!

Ah, little dreams the quiet dame
Who plies with rock and spindle
The patient flax, how great a flame
Yon little spark shall kindle!

The lurid morning shall reveal
A fire no king can smother
Where British flint and Boston steel
Have clashed against each other!

Old charters shrivel in its track,
His Worship's bench has crumbled,
It climbs and clasps the Union-Jack,
Its blazoned pomp is humbled,

The flags go down on land and sea
Like corn before the reapers;
So burned the fire that brewed the tea
That Boston served her keepers!

The waves that wrought a century's wreck
Have rolled o'er whig and tory;
The Mohawks on the *Dartmouth*'s deck
Still live in song and story;

continues

The waters in the rebel bay
Have kept the tea-leaf savor;
Our old North-Enders in their spray
Still taste a Hyson flavor;

And Freedom's teacup still o'erflows
With ever fresh libations,
To cheat of slumber all her foes
And cheer the wakening nations!

The Liberty Song

Come join hand in hand, brave Americans all,
And rouse your bold hearts at fair Liberty's call;
No tyrannous acts shall suppress your just claim,
Or stain with dishonor America's name,
  In freedom we're born, and in freedom we'll live;
    Our purses are ready,
    Steady, Friends, steady,
  Not as slaves, but as freemen our money
    we'll give.

Our worthy forefathers—let's give them a cheer—
To climates unknown did courageously steer;
Thro' oceans to deserts, for freedom they came,
And, dying, bequeath'd us their freedom and fame.
  In freedom we're born, and in freedom we'll live;
    Our purses are ready,
    Steady, Friends, steady,
  Not as slaves, but as freemen our money
    we'll give.

The tree, their own hands had to Liberty rear'd,
They lived to behold growing strong and rever'd;
With transport then cried,—"Now our wishes
  we gain,

stanza continues

JOHN DICKINSON (1732–1808)

For our children shall gather the fruits of our pain."
In freedom we're born, and in freedom we'll live;
Our purses are ready,
Steady, Friends, steady,
Not as slaves, but as freemen our money
we'll give.

Swarms of placemen and pensioners soon will
appear
Like locusts deforming the charms of the year;
Suns vainly will rise, Showers vainly descend,
If we are to drudge for what others shall spend.
In freedom we're born, and in freedom we'll live;
Our purses are ready,
Steady, Friends, steady,
Not as slaves, but as freemen our money
we'll give.

Then join hand in hand, brave Americans all,
By uniting we stand, by dividing we fall;
In so righteous a cause let us hope to succeed,
For Heaven approves of each generous deed.
In freedom we're born, and in freedom we'll live;
Our purses are ready,
Steady, Friends, steady,
Not as slaves, but as freemen our money
we'll give.

All ages shall speak with amaze and applause,
Of the courage we'll show in support of our laws;
To die we can bear,—but to serve we disdain,
For shame is to freemen more dreadful than pain.
In freedom we're born, and in freedom we'll live;
Our purses are ready,
Steady, Friends, steady,
Not as slaves, but as freemen our money
we'll give.

This bumper I crown for our sovereign's health,
And this for Britannia's glory and wealth;
That wealth and that glory immortal may be,
If she is but just, and we are but free.
In freedom we're born, and in freedom we'll live;
Our purses are ready,
Steady, Friends, steady,
Not as slaves, but as freemen our money
we'll give.

Paul Revere's Ride

Listen, my children, and you shall hear
Of the midnight ride of Paul Revere,
On the eighteenth of April, in Seventy-five;
Hardly a man is now alive
Who remembers that famous day and year.

He said to his friend, "If the British march
By land or sea from the town to-night,
Hang a lantern aloft in the belfry arch
Of the North Church tower as a signal light,—
One if by land, and two if by sea;
And I on the opposite shore will be,
Ready to ride and spread the alarm
Through every Middlesex village and farm,
For the country folk to be up and to arm."

Then he said "Good-night!" and with muffled oar
Silently rowed to the Charlestown shore,
Just as the moon rose over the bay,
Where swinging wide at her moorings lay
The *Somerset,* British man-of-war;
A phantom ship, with each mast and spar
Across the moon like a prison bar,
And a huge black hulk, that was magnified
By its own reflection in the tide.

Meanwhile, his friend through alley and street
Wanders and watches, with eager ears,
Till in the silence around him he hears
The muster of men at the barrack door,
The sound of arms, and the tramp of feet,
And the measured tread of the grenadiers,
Marching down to their boats on the shore.

Then he climbed the tower of the Old North
  Church,
By the wooden stairs, with stealthy tread,
To the belfry chamber overhead,
And startled the pigeons from their perch
On the sombre rafters, that round him made
Masses and moving shapes of shade, —
By the trembling ladder, steep and tall,
To the highest window in the wall,
Where he paused to listen and look down
A moment on the roofs of the town
And the moonlight flowing over all.

Beneath, in the churchyard, lay the dead,
In their night encampment on the hill,
Wrapped in silence so deep and still
That he could hear, like a sentinel's tread,
The watchful night-wind, as it went
Creeping along from tent to tent,

stanza continues

And seeming to whisper, "All is well!"
A moment only he feels the spell
Of the place and the hour, and the secret dread
Of the lonely belfry and the dead;
For suddenly all his thoughts are bent
On a shadowy something far away,
Where the river widens to meet the bay,—
A line of black that bends and floats
On the rising tide like a bridge of boats.

Meanwhile, impatient to mount and ride,
Booted and spurred, with a heavy stride
On the opposite shore walked Paul Revere.
Now he patted his horse's side,
Now he gazed at the landscape far and near,
Then, impetuous, stamped the earth,
And turned and tightened his saddle girth;
But mostly he watched with eager search
The belfry tower of the Old North Church,
As it rose above the graves on the hill,
Lonely and spectral and sombre and still.
And lo! as he looks, on the belfry's height
A glimmer, and then a gleam of light!
He springs to the saddle, the bridle he turns,
But lingers and gazes, till full on his sight
A second lamp in the belfry burns.

A hurry of hoofs in a village street,
A shape in the moonlight, a bulk in the dark,
And beneath, from the pebbles, in passing, a spark
Struck out by a steed flying fearless and fleet;
That was all! And yet, through the gloom and
  the light,
The fate of a nation was riding that night;
And the spark struck out by that steed, in
  his flight,
Kindled the land into flame with its heat.
He has left the village and mounted the steep,
And beneath him, tranquil and broad and deep,
Is the Mystic, meeting the ocean tides;
And under the alders that skirt its edge,
Now soft on the sand, now loud on the ledge,
Is heard the tramp of his steed as he rides.

It was twelve by the village clock
When he crossed the bridge into Medford town.
He heard the crowing of the cock,
And the barking of the farmer's dog,
And felt the damp of the river fog,
That rises after the sun goes down.

It was one by the village clock,
When he galloped into Lexington.

stanza continues

He saw the gilded weathercock
Swim in the moonlight as he passed,
And the meeting-house windows, black and bare,
Gaze at him with a spectral glare,
As if they already stood aghast
At the bloody work they would look upon.

It was two by the village clock,
When he came to the bridge in Concord town.
He heard the bleating of the flock,
And the twitter of birds among the trees,
And felt the breath of the morning breeze
Blowing over the meadow brown.
And one was safe and asleep in his bed
Who at the bridge would be first to fall,
Who that day would be lying dead,
Pierced by a British musket ball.

You know the rest. In the books you have read
How the British Regulars fired and fled,—
How the farmers gave them ball for ball,
From behind each fence and farmyard wall,
Chasing the redcoats down the lane,
Then crossing the fields to emerge again
Under the trees at the turn of the road,
And only pausing to fire and load.

So through the night rode Paul Revere;
And so through the night went his cry of alarm
To every Middlesex village and farm,—
A cry of defiance, and not of fear,
A voice in the darkness, a knock at the door,
And a word that shall echo for evermore!
For, borne on the night-wind of the Past,
Through all our history, to the last,
In the hour of darkness and peril and need,
The people will waken and listen to hear
The hurrying hoof-beats of that steed,
And the midnight message of Paul Revere.

Grandmother's Story of Bunker-Hill Battle

'Tis like stirring living embers when, at eighty, one
 remembers
All the achings and the quakings of "the times that
 tried men's souls;"
When I talk of *Whig* and *Tory,* when I tell the *Rebel*
 story,
To you the words are ashes, but to me they're
 burning coals.

I had heard the muskets' rattle of the April
 running battle;
Lord Percy's hunted soldiers, I can see their red
 coats still;
But a deadly chill comes o'er me, as the day looms
 up before me,
When a thousand men lay bleeding on the slopes
 of Bunker's Hill.

'T was a peaceful summer's morning, when the
 first thing gave us warning
Was the booming of the cannon from the river and
 the shore:

stanza continues

"Child," says grandma, "what's the matter, what is
all this noise and clatter?
Have those scalping Indian devils come to murder
us once more?"

Poor old soul! my sides were shaking in the midst
of all my quaking,
To hear her talk of Indians when the guns began to
roar:
She had seen the burning village, and the slaughter
and the pillage,
When the Mohawks killed her father with their
bullets through his door.

Then I said, "Now, dear old granny, don't you fret
and worry any,
For I'll soon come back and tell you whether this is
work or play;
There can't be mischief in it, so I won't be gone a
minute"—
For a minute then I started. I was gone the
livelong day.

No time for bodice-lacing or for looking-glass
grimacing;
Down my hair went as I hurried, tumbling half-
way to my heels;

stanza continues

God forbid your ever knowing, when there's blood around her flowing,
How the lonely, helpless daughter of a quiet household feels!

In the street I heard a thumping; and I knew it was the stumping
Of the Corporal, our old neighbor, on that wooden leg he wore,
With a knot of women round him,—it was lucky I had found him,
So I followed with the others, and the Corporal marched before.

They were making for the steeple,—the old soldier and his people;
The pigeons circled round us as we climbed the creaking stair.
Just across the narrow river—oh, so close it made me shiver!—
Stood a fortress on the hill-top that but yesterday was bare.

Not slow our eyes to find it; well we knew who stood behind it,
Though the earthwork hid them from us, and the stubborn walls were dumb:

stanza continues

Here were sister, wife, and mother, looking wild
upon each other,
And their lips were white with terror as they said,
THE HOUR HAS COME!

The morning slowly wasted, not a morsel had we
tasted,
And our heads were almost splitting with the
cannons' deafening thrill,
When a figure tall and stately round the rampart
strode sedately;
It was PRESCOTT, one since told me; he
commanded on the hill.

Every woman's heart grew bigger when we saw his
manly figure,
With the banyan buckled round it, standing up so
straight and tall;
Like a gentleman of leisure who is strolling out for
pleasure,
Through the storm of shells and cannon-shot he
walked around the wall.

At eleven the streets were swarming, for the
redcoats' ranks were forming;
At noon in marching order they were moving to
the piers;

stanza continues

How the bayonets gleamed and glistened, as we
looked far down, and listened
To the trampling and the drum-beat of the belted
grenadiers!

At length the men have started, with a cheer (it
seemed faint-hearted),
In their scarlet regimentals, with their knapsacks
on their backs,
And the reddening, rippling water, as after a sea-
fight's slaughter,
Round the barges gliding onward blushed like
blood along their tracks.

So they crossed to the other border, and again they
formed in order;
And the boats came back for soldiers, came for
soldiers, soldiers still:
The time seemed everlasting to us women faint and
fasting,—
At last they're moving, marching, marching
proudly up the hill.

We can see the bright steel glancing all along the
lines advancing,—
Now the front rank fires a volley,—they have
thrown away their shot;

stanza continues

For behind their earthwork lying, all the balls
above them flying,
Our people need not hurry; so they wait and
answer not.

Then the Corporal, our old cripple (he would
swear sometimes and tipple), —
He had heard the bullets whistle (in the old French
war) before, —
Calls out in words of jeering, just as if they all
were hearing, —
And his wooden leg thumps fiercely on the dusty
belfry floor: —

"Oh! fire away, ye villains, and earn King George's
shillin's,
But ye'll waste a ton of powder afore a 'rebel' falls;
You may bang the dirt and welcome, they're as
safe as Dan'l Malcolm
Ten foot beneath the gravestone that you've
splintered with your balls!"

In the hush of expectation, in the awe and
trepidation
Of the dread approaching moment, we are well-
nigh breathless all;

stanza continues

Though the rotten bars are failing on the rickety belfry railing,
We are crowding up against them like the waves against a wall.

Just a glimpse (the air is clearer), they are nearer,—nearer,—nearer,
When a flash—a curling smoke-wreath—then a crash—the steeple shakes—
The deadly truce is ended; the tempest's shroud is rended;
Like a morning mist it gathered, like a thundercloud it breaks!

Oh the sight our eyes discover as the blue-black smoke blows over!
The red-coats stretched in windrows as a mower rakes his hay;
Here a scarlet heap is lying, there a headlong crowd is flying
Like a billow that has broken and is shivered into spray.

Then we cried, "The troops are routed! they are beat—it can't be doubted!
God be thanked, the fight is over!"—Ah! the grim old soldier's smile!

stanza continues

"Tell us, tell us why you look so?" (we could
  hardly speak, we shook so), —
"Are they beaten? *Are* they beaten? ARE they
  beaten?" — "Wait a while."

Oh the trembling and the terror! for too soon we
  saw our error:
They are baffled, not defeated; we have driven
  them back in vain;
And the columns that were scattered, round the
  colors that were tattered,
Toward the sullen, silent fortress turn their belted
  breasts again.

All at once, as we are gazing, lo the roofs of
  Charlestown blazing!
They have fired the harmless village; in an hour it
  will be down!
The Lord in heaven confound them, rain his fire
  and brimstone round them, —
The robbing, murdering red-coats, that would
  burn a peaceful town!

They are marching, stern and solemn; we can see
  each massive column
As they near the naked earth-mound with the
  slanting walls so steep.

stanza continues

Have our soldiers got faint-hearted, and in
  noiseless haste departed?
Are they panic-struck and helpless? Are they
  palsied or asleep?

Now! the walls they're almost under! scarce a rod
  the foes asunder!
Not a firelock flashed against them! up the
  earthwork they will swarm!
But the words have scarce been spoken, when the
  ominous calm is broken,
And a bellowing crash has emptied all the
  vengeance of the storm!

So again, with murderous slaughter, pelted
  backwards to the water,
Fly Pigot's running heroes and the frightened
  braves of Howe;
And we shout, "At last they're done for, it's their
  barges they have run for:
They are beaten, beaten, beaten; and the battle's
  over now!"

And we looked, poor timid creatures, on the rough
  old soldier's features,
Our lips afraid to question, but he knew what we
  would ask:

stanza continues

"Not sure," he said; "keep quiet,—once more, I
guess, they'll try it—
Here's damnation to the cut-throats!"—then he
handed me his flask,

Saying, "Gal, you're looking shaky; have a drop of
old Jamaiky;
I'm afeard there'll be more trouble afore the job is
done;"
So I took one scorching swallow; dreadful faint I
felt and hollow,
Standing there from early morning when the firing
was begun.

All through those hours of trial I had watched a
calm clock dial,
As the hands kept creeping, creeping,—they were
creeping round to four,
When the old man said, "They're forming with
their bagonets fixed for storming:
It's the death-grip that's a-coming,—they will try
the works once more."

With brazen trumpets blaring, the flames behind
them glaring,
The deadly wall before them, in close array they
come;

stanza continues

Still onward, upward toiling, like a dragon's fold uncoiling,—
Like the rattlesnake's shrill warning the reverberating drum!

Over heaps all torn and gory—shall I tell the fearful story,
How they surged above the breastwork, as a sea breaks over a deck;
How, driven, yet scarce defeated, our worn-out men retreated,
With their powder-horns all emptied, like the swimmers from a wreck?

It has all been told and painted; as for me, they say I fainted,
And the wooden-legged old Corporal stumped with me down the stair:
When I woke from dreams affrighted the evening lamps were lighted,—
On the floor a youth was lying; his bleeding breast was bare.

And I heard through all the flurry, "Send for WARREN! hurry! hurry!
Tell him here's a soldier bleeding, and he'll come and dress his wound!"

stanza continues

Ah, we knew not till the morrow told its tale of
death and sorrow,
How the starlight found him stiffened on the dark
and bloody ground.

Who the youth was, what his name was, where the
place from which he came was,
Who had brought him from the battle, and had left
him at our door,
He could not speak to tell us; but 't was one of our
brave fellows,
As the homespun plainly showed us which the
dying soldier wore.

For they all thought he was dying, as they
gathered round him crying,—
And they said, "Oh, how they'll miss him!" and,
"What *will* his mother do?"
Then, his eyelids just unclosing like a child's that
has been dozing,
He faintly murmured, "Mother!"—and—I saw his
eyes were blue.

"Why, grandma, how you're winking!" Ah, my
child, it sets me thinking
Of a story not like this one. Well, he somehow
lived along;

stanza continues

So we came to know each other, and I nursed him like a—mother,
Till at last he stood before me, tall, and rosy-cheeked, and strong.

And we sometimes walked together in the pleasant summer weather,—
"Please to tell us what his name was?" Just your own, my little dear,—
There's his picture Copley painted: we became so well acquainted,
That—in short, that's why I'm grandma, and you children all are here!

Concord Hymn

By the rude bridge that arched the flood,
Their flag to April's breeze unfurled,
Here once the embattled farmers stood,
And fired the shot heard round the world.

The foe long since in silence slept;
Alike the conqueror silent sleeps;
And Time the ruined bridge has swept
Down the dark stream which seaward creeps.

On this green bank, by this soft stream,
We set to-day a votive stone;
That memory may their deed redeem,
When, like our sires, our sons are gone.

Spirit that made those heroes dare
To die, and leave their children free,
Bid Time and Nature gently spare
The shaft we raise to them and thee.

RALPH WALDO EMERSON (1803–1882)

Independence Bell

There was tumult in the city,
  In the quaint old Quaker town,
And the streets were thronged with people
  Passing restless up and down—
People gathering at the corners,
  Where they whispered lip to ear,
While the sweat stood on their temples,
  With the stress of hope and fear.

As the bleak Atlantic currents
  Lash the wild Newfoundland shore,
So they beat about the State House,
  So they surged against the door;
And the mingling of their voices
  Swelled in harmony profound,
Till the quiet street of Chestnut
  Was all turbulent with sound.

"Will they do it?" "Dare they do it?"
  "Who is speaking?" "What's the news?"
"What of Adams?" "What of Sherman?"
  "Oh, God grant they won't refuse!"
"Make some way, there!" "Let me nearer!"
  "I am stifling!" "Stifle then!

stanza continues

When a nation's life's at hazard
  We've no time to think of men!"

So they surged against the State House,
  While all solemnly inside
Sat the Continental Congress,
  Truth and reason for their guide;
O'er a simple scroll debating:
  Which, though simple it might be,
Yet should shake the cliffs of England
  With the thunders of the free.

Far aloft in the high steeple
  Sat the bellman, old and gray;
He was weary of the tyrant
  And his iron-sceptered sway.
So he sat with one hand ready
  On the clapper of the bell,
Till his eye should catch the signal,
  The expected news to tell.

See! See! the dense crowd quivers
  As beside the door a boy
Looks forth with hands uplifted,
  His eyes alight with joy.

stanza continues

Hushed the people's swelling murmur
  As they listen breathlessly—
"Ring!" he shouts; "ring, grandpa, ring!
  Ring! oh, ring for liberty!"

Quickly at the welcome signal
  The old bellman lifts his hand;
Forth he sends the good news, making
  Iron music through the land.
How they shouted! What rejoicing!
  How the old bell shook the air,
Till the clang of freedom echoed
  From the belfries everywhere.

The old State House bell is silent,
  Hushed is now its clamorous tongue,
But the spirit it awakened
  Still is living, ever young.
And we'll ne'er forget the bellman
  Who, that great day in July,
Hailed the birth of Independence,
  Which, please God, shall never die.

Betsy's Battle Flag

From dusk till dawn the livelong night
She kept the tallow dips alight,
And fast her nimble fingers flew
To sew the stars upon the blue.
With weary eyes and aching head
She stitched the stripes of white and red,
And when the day came up the stair
Complete across a carven chair
  Hung Betsy's battle flag.

Like shadows in the evening gray
The Continentals filed away,
With broken boots and ragged coats,
But hoarse defiance in their throats;
They bore the marks of want and cold,
And some were lame and some were old,
And some with wounds untended bled,
But floating bravely overhead
  Was Betsy's battle flag.

When fell the battle's leaden rain,
The solider hushed his moans of pain
And raised his dying head to see
King George's troopers turn and flee.

stanza continues

Their charging column reeled and broke,
And vanished in the rolling smoke,
Before the glory of the stars,
The snowy stripes, and scarlet bars
  Of Betsy's battle flag.

The simple stone of Betsy Ross
Is covered now with mold and moss,
But still her deathless banner flies,
And keeps the color of the skies.
A nation thrills, a nation bleeds,
A nation follows where it leads,
And every man is proud to yield
His life upon a crimson field
  For Betsy's battle flag!

MINNA IRVING (LATE 19TH CENTURY)

Nathan Hale

To drum-beat and heart-beat,
A soldier marches by;
There is color in his cheek,
There is courage in his eye,
Yet to the drum-beat and heart-beat
In a moment he must die.

By starlight and moonlight,
He seeks the Briton's camp;
He hears the rustling flag
And the armed sentry's tramp;
And the starlight and moonlight
His silent wandering's lamp.

With slow tread and still tread,
He scans the tented line;
And he counts the battery guns,
By the gaunt and shadowy pine;
And his slow tread and still tread
Gives no warning sign.

The dark wave, the plumed wave,
It meets his eager glance;
And it sparkles 'neath the stars,

stanza continues

Like the glimmer of a lance—
A dark wave, a plumed wave,
On an emerald expanse.

A sharp clang, a still clang,
And terror in the sound!
For the sentry, falcon-eyed,
In the camp a spy hath found;
With a sharp clang, a steel clang,
The patriot is bound.

With calm brow, and steady brow,
He listens to his doom;
In his look there is no fear,
Nor a shadow-trace of gloom;
But with calm brow and steady brow,
He robes him for the tomb.

In the long night, the still night,
He kneels upon the sod;
And the brutal guards withhold
E'en the solemn word of God!
In the long night, the still night,
He walks where Christ hath trod.

'Neath the blue morn, the sunny morn,
He dies upon the tree;

stanza continues

And he mourns that he can lose
But one life for Liberty;
And in the blue morn, the sunny morn,
His spirit wings are free.

But his last words, his message-words,
They burn, lest friendly eye
Should read how proud and calm
A patriot could die,
With his last words, his dying words,
A soldier's battle-cry.

From Fame-leaf and Angel-leaf,
From monument and urn,
The sad of earth, the glad of heaven,
His tragic fate shall learn;
But on Fame-leaf and Angel-leaf
The name of HALE shall burn!

Seventy-Six

What heroes from the woodland sprung,
  When, through the fresh-awakened land,
The thrilling cry of freedom rung
And to the work of warfare strung
  The yeoman's iron hand!

Hills flung the cry to hills around,
  And ocean-mart replied to mart,
And streams, whose springs were yet unfound,
Pealed far away the startling sound
  Into the forest's heart.

Then marched the brave from rocky steep,
  From mountain-river swift and cold;
The borders of the stormy deep,
The vales where gathered waters sleep,
  Sent up the strong and bold,—

As if the very earth again
  Grew quick with God's creating breath,
And, from the sods of grove and glen,
Rose ranks of lion-hearted men
  To battle to the death.

The wife, whose babe first smiled that day,
  The fair fond bride of yestereve,
And agèd sire and matron gray,
Saw the loved warriors haste away,
  And deemed it sin to grieve.

Already had the strife begun;
  Already blood, on Concord's plain,
Along the springing grass had run,
And blood had flowed at Lexington,
  Like brooks of April rain.

That death-stain on the vernal sward
  Hallowed to freedom all the shore;
In fragments fell the yoke abhorred—
The footstep of a foreign lord
  Profaned the soil no more.

Molly Pitcher

'Twas hurry and scurry at Monmouth Town,
  For Lee was beating a wild retreat;
The British were riding the Yankees down,
  And panic was pressing on flying fleet.

Galloping down like a hurricane
  Washington rode with his sword swung high,
Mighty as he of the Trojan plain
  Fired by a courage from the sky.

"Halt, and stand to your guns!" he cried.
  And a bombardier made swift reply.
Wheeling his cannon into the tide,
  He fell 'neath the shot of a foeman nigh.

Molly Pitcher sprang to his side,
  Fired as she saw her husband do.
Telling the king in his stubborn pride
  Women like men to their homes are true.

Washington rode from the bloody fray
  Up to the gun that a woman manned.
"Molly Pitcher, you saved the day,"
  He said, as he gave her a hero's hand.

He named her sergeant with manly praise,
  While her war-brown face was wet with tears—
A woman has ever a woman's ways,
  And the army was wild with cheers.

The Vow of Washington

The sword was sheathed: in April's sun
Lay green the fields by Freedom won;
And severed sections, weary of debates,
Joined hands at last and were United States.

O City sitting by the Sea!
How proud the day that dawned on thee,
When the new era, long desired, began,
And, in its need, the hour had found the man!

One thought the cannon salvos spoke,
The resonant bell-tower's vibrant stroke,
The voiceful streets, the plaudit-echoing halls,
And prayer and hymn borne heavenward from
Saint Paul's!

How felt the land in every part
The strong throb of a nation's heart,
As its great leader gave, with reverent awe,
His pledge to Union, Liberty, and Law!

That pledge the heavens above him heard,
That vow the sleep of centuries stirred;
In world-wide wonder listening peoples bent
Their gaze on Freedom's great experiment.

Could it succeed? Of honor sold
And hopes deceived all history told.
Above the wrecks that strewed the mournful past,
Was the long dream of ages true at last?

Thank God! the people's choice was just,
The one man equal to his trust,
Wise beyond lore, and without weakness good,
Calm in the strength of flawless rectitude!

His rule of justice, order, peace,
Made possible the world's release;
Taught prince and serf that power is but a trust,
And rule alone, which serves the ruled, is just;

That Freedom generous is, but strong
In hate of fraud and selfish wrong,
Pretence that turns her holy truth to lies,
And lawless license masking in her guise.

Land of his love! with one glad voice
Let thy great sisterhood rejoice;
A century's suns o'er thee have risen and set
And, God be praised, we are one nation yet.

And still we trust the years to be
Shall prove his hope was destiny,

stanza continues

Leaving our flag, with all its added stars,
Unrent by faction and unstained by wars.

Lo! where with patient toil he nursed
And trained the new-set plant at first,
The widening branches of a stately tree
Stretch from the sunrise to the sunset sea.

And in its broad and sheltering shade,
Sitting with none to make afraid,
Were we now silent, through each mighty limb,
The winds of heaven would sing the praise of
him. . . .

The Star-Spangled Banner

O say, can you see, by the dawn's early light,
What so proudly we hailed at the twilight's last gleaming?
Whose broad stripes and bright stars, through the perilous fight,
O'er the ramparts we watched, were so gallantly streaming!
And the rockets' red glare, the bombs bursting in air,
Gave proof through the night that our flag was still there:
O say, does that star-spangled banner yet wave
O'er the land of the free and the home of the brave?

On the shore, dimly seen through the mists of the deep,
Where the foe's haughty host in dread silence reposes,
What is that which the breeze, o'er the towering steep,
As it fitfully blows, now conceals, now discloses?
Now it catches the gleam of the morning's first beam,

stanza continues

In full glory reflected now shines on the stream:
'Tis the star-spangled banner! O long may it wave
O'er the land of the free and the home of the brave!

And where is that band who so vauntingly swore
That the havoc of war and the battle's confusion
A home and a country should leave us no more?
Their blood has washed out their foul footsteps' pollution.
No refuge could save the hireling and slave
From the terror of flight, or the gloom of the grave:
And the star-spangled banner in triumph doth wave
O'er the land of the free and the home of the brave!

Oh! thus be it ever, when freemen shall stand
Between their loved homes and the war's desolation!
Blest with victory and peace, may the heaven-rescued land
Praise the Power that hath made and preserved us a nation.
Then conquer we must, for our cause it is just,
And this be our motto: "In God is our trust."
And the star-spangled banner in triumph shall wave
O'er the land of the free and the home of the brave!

Justice: An Ode

I

Child of the dust! to yonder skies
  Thy vision canst thou turn?
And trace with perishable eyes,
  The seats where seraphs burn?
There, by the throne of God on high,
An angel form canst thou descry,
  Ineffably sublime?
Or is the effulgence of the Light,
Intense, insufferably bright,
  For beings born of Time?

II

That angel form, in light enshrined,
  Beside the living throne,
Is Justice, still to heaven confined—
  For God is just alone.
This Angel, of celestial birth,
Her faint resemblance here on earth
  Has sent, mankind to guide—
Yet, though obscured her brightest beams,
Still with too vivid ray she gleams
  For Mortals to abide.

continues

III

When the first father of our race
  Against his God rebelled,
Was banished from his Maker's face,
  From Paradise expelled;
For guilt unbounded to atone,
What bound could punishment have known,
  Had Justice dealt the blow?
Sure, to infernal regions hurled,
His doom had been a flaming world
  Of never ending woe!

IV

But Mercy, from the throne of God,
  Extended forth her hand;
Withheld th' exterminating rod,
  And quenched the flaming brand:
His blood the blest Redeemer gave,
Th' apostate victim's blood to save,
  And fill redemption's plan:
Angels proclaimed in choral songs,
"Justice to God alone belongs,
  And Mercy pardons man."

V

When, issuing from the savage wild,
  Man forms the social tie,
Justice severe, and Mercy mild,
  To bind the compact vie;
Of each his own, the parting hedge
Stern Justice takes the solemn pledge;
  The sacred vow enjoins.
While Mercy, with benignant face,
Bids man his fellow-man embrace,
  And heart with heart entwines.

VI

To both united is the trust
  Of human laws consigned;
One teaches mortals to be just;
  The other, to be kind;
Yet shall not Justice always wear
The garb of punishment, or bear
  The avenging sword to smite:
Nor Mercy's ever gladdening eye
Permit the ruffian to defy
  Th' unerring rule of right.

continues

VII

To Justice, dearer far the part
  To tune the plausive voice;
Of Virtue to delight the heart,
  And bid the good rejoice.
To yield the meed of grateful praise—
The deathless monument to raise,
  To honor Virtue dead;
Or wreathe the chaplet of renown,
The laurel or the mural crown,
  For living Virtue's head.

VIII

Here, to defend his native land,
  His sword the patriot draws;
Here the mock hero lifts his hand
  To aid a tyrant's cause.
When, meeting on the field of blood
They pour the sanguinary flood,
  Whose triumph waves unfurled?
Alas! let Cheronea tell;
Or plains where godlike Brutus fell.
  Or Cæsar won the world!

IX

In arms, when hostile nations rise
  And blood the strife decides,
'Tis brutal force awards the prize,
  Her head while Justice hides.
But short is force's triumph base:
Justice unveils her awful face,
  And hurls him from the steep;
Strips from his brow the wreath of fame,
And after ages load his name
  With curses loud and deep.

X

Behold the lettered sage devote
  The labors of his mind,
His country's welfare to promote,
  And benefit mankind.
Lo! from the blackest caves of hell,
A phalanx fierce of monsters fell,
  Combine their fearful bands—
His fame asperse, his toils assail;
Till Justice holds aloft her scale
  And shields him from their hands.

continues

XI

Of excellence, in every clime,
'Tis thus the lot is cast;
Passion usurps the present time,
But Justice rules the past:
Envy, and selfishness, and pride,
The passing hours of man divide
With unresisted sway;
But Justice comes, with noiseless tread,
O'ertakes the filmy spider's thread
And sweeps the net away.

XII

Eternal Spirit! Lord supreme
Of blessing and of woe!
Of Justice, ever living stream!
Whose mercies ceaseless flow—
Make me, while earth shall be my span,
Just to my fellow-mortal, man,
Whate'er my lot may be.
And when this transient scene is o'er,
Pure let my deathless spirit soar,
And Mercy find from thee.

The Death of Jefferson

I

'Twas midsummer; cooling breezes all the languid
forests fanned,
And the angel of the evening drew her curtain o'er
the land.
Like an isle rose Monticello through the cooled
and rippling trees,
Like an isle in rippling starlight in the silence of
the seas.
Ceased the mocking-bird his singing; said the
slaves with faltering breath,
" 'Tis the Third, and on the morrow Heaven will
send the Angel Death."

II

In his room at Monticello, lost in dreams the
statesman slept,
Seeing not the still forms round him, seeing not the
eyes that wept,
Hearing not the old clock ticking in life's final
silence loud,
Knowing not when night came o'er him like the
shadow of a cloud.

stanza continues

In the past his soul is living as in fifty years ago,
Hastes again to Philadelphia, hears again the
  Schuylkill flow—

III

Meets again the elder Adams—knowing not that
  far away
He is waiting for Death's morrow, on old
  Massachusetts Bay;
Meets with Hancock, young and courtly, meets
  with Hopkins, bent and old,
Meets again calm Roger Sherman, fiery Lee, and
  Carroll bold,
Meets the sturdy form of Franklin, meets the half a
  hundred men
Who have made themselves immortal,—breathes
  the ancient morn again.

IV

Once again the Declaration in his nerveless hands
  he holds,
And before the waiting statesmen its prophetic
  hope unfolds,—
Reads again the words puissant, "All men are
  created free,"
Claims again for man his birthright, claims the
  world's equality;

stanza continues

Hears the coming and the going of an hundred
firm-set feet,
Hears the summer breezes blowing 'mid the oak
trees cool and sweet.

V

Sees again tall Patrick Henry by the side of Henry
Lee,
Hears him cry, "And will ye sign it?—it will make
all nations free!
Fear ye not the axe or gibbet; it shall topple every
throne.
Sign it for the world's redemption!—all mankind
its truth shall own!
Stars may fall, but truth eternal shall not falter,
shall not fail.
Sign it, and the Declaration shall the voice of ages
hail."

VI

"Sign, and set yon dumb bell ringing, that the
people all may know
Man has found emancipation; sign, the Almighty
wills it so."
Sees one sign it, then another, till like magic moves
the pen,

stanza continues

Till all have signed it, and it lies there, Charter of
the rights of men.
Hears the small bells, hears the great bell, hanging
idly in the sun,
Break the silence, and the people whisper, awe-
struck, "It is done."

VII

Then the dream began to vanish—burgesses, the
war's red flames,
Charging Tarleton, proud Cornwallis, navies
moving on the James,
Years of peace, and years of glory, all began to
melt away,
And the statesman woke from slumber in the night,
and tranquil lay,
And his lips moved; friends there gathered with
love's silken footstep near,
And he whispered, softly whispered in love's low
and tender ear,—

VIII

"It is the Fourth?" "No, not yet," they answered,
"but 't will soon be early morn;
We will wake you, if you slumber, when the day
begins to dawn."

stanza continues

Then the statesman left the present, lived again
amid the past,
Saw, perhaps, the peopled future ope its portals
grand and vast,
Till the flashes of the morning lit the far horizon low,
And the sun's rays o'er the forests in the east began
to glow.

IX

Rose the sun, and from the woodlands, fell the
midnight dews like rain,
In magnolias cool and shady sang the mocking-
bird again;
And the statesman woke from slumber, saw the
risen sun, and heard
Rippling breezes 'mid the oak trees, and the lattice
singing bird,
And, his eye serene uplifted, as rejoicing in the sun,
"It is the Fourth?" his only question,—to the world
his final one.

X

Silence fell on Monticello—for the last dread hour
was near,
And the old clock's measured ticking only broke
upon the ear.

stanza continues

All the summer rooms were silent, where the great of earth had trod,
All the summer blooms seemed silent as the messengers of God;
Silent were the hall and chamber where old councils oft had met,
Save the far boom of the cannon that recalled the old day yet.

XI

Silent still is Monticello—he is breathing slowly now,
In the splendors of the noon-tide, with the death-dew on his brow—
Silent save the clock still ticking where his soul had given birth
To the mighty thoughts of freedom, that should free the fettered earth;
Silent save the boom of cannon on the sun-filled wave afar,
Bringing 'mid the peace eternal still the memory of war.

XII

Evening in majestic shadows fell upon the fortress' walls;
Sweetly were the last bells ringing on the James and on the Charles.
'Mid the choruses of freedom two departed victors lay,
One beside the blue Rivanna, one by Massachusetts Bay.
He was gone, and night her sable curtain drew across the sky;
Gone his soul into all nations, gone to live and not to die.

La Fayette

Born, nurtured, wedded, prized, within the pale
Of peers and princes, high in camp—at court—
He hears, in joyous youth, a wild report,
Swelling the murmurs of the Western gale,
Of a young people struggling to be free!
Straight quitting all, across the wave he flies,
Aids with his sword, wealth, blood, the high
  emprize!
And shares the glories of its victory.
Then comes for fifty years a high romance
Of toils, reverses, sufferings, in the cause
Of man and justice, liberty and France,
Crowned, at the last, with hope and wide applause.
Champion of Freedom! Well thy race was run!
All time shall hail three, Europe's noblest Son!

Old Ironsides

Ay, tear her tattered ensign down!
  Long has it waved on high,
And many an eye has danced to see
  That banner in the sky;
Beneath it rung the battle shout,
  And burst the cannon's roar;—
The meteor of the ocean air
  Shall sweep the clouds no more.

Her deck, once red with heroes' blood,
  Where knelt the vanquished foe,
When winds were hurrying o'er the flood,
  And waves were white below,
No more shall feel the victor's tread,
  Or know the conquered knee;—
The harpies of the shore shall pluck
  The eagle of the sea!

Oh, better that her shattered hulk
  Should sink beneath the wave;
Her thunders shook the mighty deep,
  And there should be her grave;
Nail to the mast her holy flag,
  Set every threadbare sail,
And give her to the god of storms,
  The lightning and the gale!

OLIVER WENDELL HOLMES (1809–1894)

Farther

Far-off a young State rises, full of might:
  I paint its brave escutcheon. Near at hand
  See the log cabin in the rough clearing stand;
A woman by its door, with steadfast sight,
Trustful, looks Westward, where, uplifted bright,
  Some city's Apparition, weird and grand,
  In dazzling quiet fronts the lonely land,
With vast and marvelous structures wrought
    of light,
Motionless on the burning cloud afar: —
  The haunting vision of a time to be,
After the heroic age is ended here,
Built on the boundless, still horizon's bar
  By the low sun, his gorgeous prophecy
Lighting the doorway of the pioneer!

JOHN JAMES PIATT (1835–1917)

Daniel Boone

Daniel Boone at twenty-one
Came with his tomahawk, knife and gun
Home from the French and Indian War
To North Carolina and the Yadkin shore.
He married his maid with a golden band,
Builded his house and cleared his land;
But the deep woods claimed their son again
And he turned his face from the homes of men.
Over the Blue Ridge, dark and lone,
The Mountains of Iron, the Hills of Stone,
Braving the Shawnee's jealous wrath,
He made his way on the Warrior's Path.
Alone he trod the shadowed trails;
But he was the lord of a thousand vales
As he roved Kentucky, far and near,
Hunting the buffalo, elk and deer.
What joy to see, what joy to win
So fair a land for his kith and kin,
Of streams unstained and woods unhewn!
"Elbowroom!" laughed Daniel Boone.

On the Wilderness Road that his axmen made
The settlers flocked to the first stockade;

stanza continues

ARTHUR GUITERMAN (1871–1943)

The deerskin shirts and the coonskin caps
Filed through the glens and the mountains gaps;
And hearts were high in the fateful spring
When the land said "Nay!" to the stubborn king.
While the men of the East of farm and town
Strove with the troops of the British Crown,
Daniel Boone from a surge of hate
Guarded a nation's westward gate.
Down on the fort in a wave of flame
The Shawnee horde and the Mingo came,
And the stout logs shook in a storm of lead;
But Boone stood firm and the savage fled.
Peace! And the settlers flocked anew,
The farm lands spread, the town lands grew;
But Daniel Boone was ill at ease
When he saw the smoke in his forest trees.
"There'll be no game in the country soon.
Elbowroom!" cried Daniel Boone.

Straight as a pine at sixty-five—
Time enough for a man to thrive—
He launched his bateau on Ohio's breast
And his heart was glad as he oared it west;
There were kindly folk and his own true blood
Where great Missouri rolls his flood;
New woods, new streams and room to spare,

stanza continues

And Daniel Boone found comfort there.
Yet far he ranged toward the sunset still,
Where the Kansas runs and the Smoky Hill,
And the prairies toss, by the south wind blown;
And he killed his bear on the Yellowstone.
But ever he dreamed of new domains
With vaster woods and wider plains;
Ever he dreamed of a world-to-be
Where there are no bounds and the soul is free.
At four-score-five, still stout and hale,
He heard a call to a farther trail;
So he turned his face where the stars are strewn;
"Elbowroom!" sighed Daniel Boone.

Down the Milky Way in its banks of blue
Far he has paddled his white canoe
To the splendid quest of the tameless soul—
He has reached the goal where there is no goal.
Now he rides and rides an endless trail
On the Hippogriff of the flaming tail
Or the Horse of the Stars with the golden mane,
As he rode the first of the blue-grass strain.
The joy that lies in the Search he seeks
On breathless hills with crystal peaks;
He makes his camp on heights untrod,
The steps of the Shrine, alone with God.

stanza continues

Through the woods of the vast, on the plains
of Space
He hunts the pride of the Mammoth race
And the Dinosaur of the triple horn,
The manticore and the Unicorn,
As once by the broad Missouri's flow
He followed the elk and the buffalo.
East of the Sun and west of the Moon,
"Elbowroom!" laughs Daniel Boone.

The Defence of the Alamo

Santa Ana came storming, as a storm might come;
There was rumble of cannon; there was rattle of blade;
There was cavalry, infantry, bugle and drum,—
Full seven thousand, in pomp and parade,
The chivalry, flower of Mexico;
And a gaunt two hundred in the Alamo!

And thirty lay sick, and some were shot through;
For the siege had been bitter, and bloody, and long.
"Surrender, or die!"—"Men, what will *you* do?"
And Travis, great Travis, drew sword, quick and strong;
Drew a line at his feet . . . "Will you come? Will you go?
I die with my wounded, in the Alamo."

The Bowie gasped, "Lead me over that line!"
Then Crockett, one hand to the sick, one hand to his gun,
Crossed with him; then never a word or a sign
Till all, sick or well, all, all save but one,
One man. Then a woman stepped, praying, and slow
Across; to die at her post in the Alamo.

continues

JOAQUIN MILLER (1841–1913)

Then that one coward fled, in the night, in that
night
When all men silently prayed and thought
Of home; of to-morrow; of God and the right,
Till dawn: and with dawn came Travis's cannon-
shot,
In answer to insolent Mexico,
From the old bell-tower of the Alamo.

Then came Santa Ana; a crescent of flame!
Then the red escalade; then the fight hand
to hand;
Such an unequal fight as never had name
Since the Persian hordes butchered that doomed
Spartan band.
All day—all day and all night; and the morning?
so slow,
Through the battle-smoke mantling the Alamo.

Now silence! Such silence! Two thousand lay dead
In a crescent outside! And within? Not a
breath
Save the gasp of a woman, with gory gashed
head,
All alone, all alone there, waiting for death;
And she but a nurse. Yet when shall we know
Another like this of the Alamo?

Shout "Victory, victory, victory ho!"
  I say 'tis not always to the hosts that win!
I say that the victory, high or low,
  Is given the hero who grapples with sin,
Or legion or single; just asking to know
When duty fronts death in his Alamo.

JOAQUIN MILLER (1841–1913)

A Tale of the Airly Days

Oh! tell me a tale of the airly days—
  Of the times as they ust to be;
"Piller of Fi-er" and "Shakespeare's Plays"
  Is a'most too deep fer me!
I want plane facts, and I want plane words,
  Of the good old-fashioned ways,
When speech run free as the songs of birds
  'Way back in the airly days.

Tell me a tale of the timber-lands—
  Of the old-time pioneers;
Somepin' a pore man understands
  With his feelin's 's well as ears.
Tell of the old log house,—about
  The loft, and the puncheon flore—
The old fi-er-place, with the crane swung out,
  And the latch-string thrugh the door.

Tell of the things jest as they was—
  They don't need no excuse!—
Don't tetch 'em up like the poets does,
  Tel theyr all too fine fer use!—
Say they was 'leven in the fambily—
  Two beds, and the chist, below,
And the trundle-beds that each helt three,
  And the clock and the old bureau.

Then blow the horn at the old back-door
  Tel the echoes all halloo,
And the childern gethers home onc't more,
  Jest as they ust to do:
Blow fer Pap tel he hears and comes,
  With Tomps and Elias, too,
A-marchin' home, with the fife and drums
  And the old Red White and Blue!

Blow and blow tel the sound draps low
  As the moan of the whipperwill,
And wake up Mother, and Ruth and Jo,
  All sleepin' at Bethel Hill:
Blow and call tel the faces all
  Shine out in the back-log's blaze,
And the shadders dance on the old hewed wall
  As they did in the airly days.

from The Prairies

These are the gardens of the Desert, these
The unshorn fields, boundless and beautiful,
For which the speech of England has no name—
The Prairies. I behold them for the first,
And my heart swells, while the dilated sight
Takes in the encircling vastness. Lo! they stretch,
In airy undulations, far away,
As if the ocean, in his gentlest swell,
Stood still, with all his rounded billows fixed,
And motionless forever.—Motionless?—
No—they are all unchained again. The clouds
Sweep over with their shadows, and, beneath,
The surface rolls and fluctuates to the eye;
Dark hollows seem to glide along and chase
The sunny ridges. Breezes of the South!
Who toss the golden and the flame-like flowers.
And pass the prairie-hawk that, poised on high,
Flaps his broad wings, yet moves not—ye
 have played
Among the palms of Mexico and vines
Of Texas, and have crisped the limpid brooks
That from the fountains of Sonora glide
Into the calm Pacific—have ye fanned
A nobler or a lovelier scene than this?
Man hath no power in all this glorious work:

The hand that built the firmament hath heaved
And smoothed these verdant swells, and sown
  their slopes
With herbage, planted them with island groves,
And hedged them round with forests. Fitting floor
For this magnificent temple of the sky—
With flowers whose glory and whose multitude
Rival the constellations! The great heavens
Seem to stoop down upon the scene in love,—
A nearer vault, and of a tenderer blue,
Than that which bends above our eastern hills.

The Kansas Emigrants

We go to rear a wall of men
  On Freedom's southern line,
And plant beside the cotton-tree
  The rugged Northern pine!

We're flowing from our native hills
  As our free rivers flow;
The blessing of our Mother-land
  Is on us as we go.

We go to plant her common schools,
  On distant prairie swells,
And give the Sabbaths of the wild
  The music of her bells.

Upbearing, like the Ark of old,
  The Bible in our van,
We go to test the truth of God
  Against the fraud of man.

No pause, nor rest, save where the streams
  That feed the Kansas run,
Save where our Pilgrim gonfalon
  Shall flout the setting sun!

We'll tread the prairie as of old
  Our fathers sailed the sea,
And make the West, as they the East,
  The homestead of the free!

On Liberty and Slavery

Alas! and am I born for this,
  To wear this slavish chain?
Deprived of all created bliss,
  Through hardship, toil and pain!

How long have I in bondage lain,
  And languished to be free!
Alas! and must I still complain—
  Deprived of liberty.

Oh, Heaven! and is there no relief
  This side the silent grave—
To soothe the pain—to quell the grief
  And anguish of a slave?

Come Liberty, thou cheerful sound,
  Roll through my ravished ears!
Come, let my grief in joys be drowned,
  And drive away my fears.

Say unto foul oppression, Cease:
  Ye tyrants rage no more,
And let the joyful trump of peace,
  Now bid the vassal soar.

Soar on the pinions of that dove
  Which long has cooed for thee,
And breathed her notes from Afric's grove,
  The sound of Liberty.

Oh, Liberty! thou golden prize,
  So often sought by blood—
We crave thy sacred sun to rise,
  The gift of nature's God!

Bid Slavery hide her haggard face,
  And barbarism fly:
I scorn to see the sad disgrace
  In which enslaved I lie.

Dear Liberty! upon thy breast
  I languish to respire;
And like the Swan unto her nest,
  I'd to thy smiles retire.

Oh, blest asylum—heavenly balm!
  Unto thy boughs I flee—
And in thy shades the storm shall calm,
  With songs of Liberty!

Follow the Drinking Gourd

(Song of the Underground Railroad)

Follow the drinking gourd,
Follow the drinking gourd,
For the old man is waiting
  for to carry you to freedom
If you follow the drinking gourd.

When the sun comes back
  and the first quail calls,
Follow the drinking gourd,
For the old man is waiting
  for to carry you to freedom
If you follow the drinking gourd.

The riverbank will make a very good road,
The dead trees show you the way,
Left foot, peg foot traveling on,
Following the drinking gourd.

The river ends between two hills,
Follow the drinking gourd.
There's another river on the other side,
Follow the drinking gourd.

 TRADITIONAL FOLK SONG (19TH CENTURY)

Where the great big river meets the little river,
Follow the drinking gourd.
The old man is waiting
  for to carry you to freedom,
If you follow the drinking gourd.

God, Give Us Men!

God, give us men! A time like this demands
Strong minds, great hearts, true faith and ready
hands;
Men whom the lust of office does not kill;
Men whom the spoils of office cannot buy;
Men who possess opinions and a will;
Men who have honor; men who will not lie;
Men who can stand before a demagogue
And damn his treacherous flatteries without
winking!
Tall men, sun-crowned, who live above the fog
In public duty and in private thinking;
For while the rabble, with their thumb-worn
creeds,
Their large professions and their little deeds,
Mingle in selfish strife, lo! Freedom weeps,
Wrong rules the land and waiting Justice sleeps.

 JOSIAH GILBERT HOLLAND (1819–1881)

John Brown's Body

John Brown's body lies a-mould'ring in the grave,
John Brown's body lies a-mould'ring in the grave,
John Brown's body lies a-mould'ring in the grave,
His soul goes marching on!

Chorus:
Glory, glory! Hallelujah!
Glory, glory! Hallelujah!
Glory, glory! Hallelujah!
His soul is marching on!

He captured Harper's Ferry with his nineteen men so true,
And he frightened old Virginia till she trembled through and through.
They hung him for a traitor, themselves the traitor crew,
But his soul is marching on!

John Brown died that the slave might be free,
John Brown died that the slave might be free,
John Brown died that the slave might be free,
And his soul is marching on!

continues

C. S. HALL & T. B. BISHOP (19TH CENTURY)

The stars of Heaven are looking kindly down,
The stars of Heaven are looking kindly down,
The stars of Heaven are looking kindly down,
On the grave of old John Brown.

Now has come the glorious jubilee,
Now has come the glorious jubilee,
Now has come the glorious jubilee,
When all mankind are free.

Enlisted Today

I know the sun shines, and the lilacs are blowing,
 And summer sends kisses by beautiful May—
Oh! to see all the treasures the spring is bestowing,
 And think my boy Willie enlisted today,

It seems but a day since at twilight, low humming,
 I rocked him to sleep with his cheek upon mine,
While Robby, the four-year-old, watched for the coming
 Of father, adown the street's indistinct line.

It is many a year since my Harry departed,
 To come back no more in the twilight or dawn:
And Robby grew weary of watching, and started
 Alone on the journey his father had gone.

It is many a year—and this afternoon sitting
 At Robby's old window, I heard the band play,
And suddenly ceased dreaming over my knitting,
 To recollect Willie is twenty today.

And that, standing beside him this soft May-day morning,
 And the sun making gold of his wreathed cigar smoke,

stanza continues

ANONYMOUS (19TH CENTURY)

I saw in his sweet eyes and lips a faint warning,
  And choked down the tears when he eagerly
    spoke:

"Dear mother, you know how these Northmen are
    crowing,
  They would trample the rights of the South in
    the dust,
The boys are all fire; and they wish I were going—"
  He stopped, but his eyes said, "Oh, say if I
    must!"

I smiled on the boy, though my heart it seemed
    breaking,
  My eyes filled with tears, so I turned them away,
And answered him, "Willie, 'tis well you are
    waking—
  Go, act as you father would bid you, today!"

I sit in the window, and see the flags flying,
  And drearily list to the roll of the drum,
And smother the pain in my heart that is lying
  And bid all the fears in my bosom be dumb.

I shall sit in the window when summer is lying
  Out over the fields, and the honey-bee's hum

stanza continues

Lulls the rose at the porch from her tremulous
    sighing,
  And watch for the face of my darling to come.

And if he should fall—his young life he has given
  For freedom's sweet sake; and for me, I will pray
Once more with my Harry and Robby in Heaven
  To meet the dear boy that enlisted today.

Killed at the Ford

He is dead, the beautiful youth,
The heart of honor, the tongue of truth,
He, the life and light of us all,
Whose voice was blithe as a bugle-call,
Whom all eyes followed with one consent,
The cheer of whose laugh, and whose pleasant word,
Hushed all murmurs of discontent.

Only last night, as we rode along,
Down the dark of the mountain gap,
To visit the picket-guard at the ford,
Little dreaming of any mishap,
He was humming the words of some old song:
"Two red roses he had on his cap
And another he bore at the point of his sword."

Sudden and swift a whistling ball
Came out of a wood, and the voice was still;
Something I heard in the darkness fall,
And for a moment my blood grew chill;
I spake in a whisper, as he who speaks
In a room where some one is lying dead;
But he made no answer to what I said.

We lifted him up to his saddle again,
And through the mire and the mist and the rain
Carried him back to the silent camp,
And laid him as if asleep on his bed;
And I saw by the light of the surgeon's lamp
Two white roses upon his cheeks,
And one, just over his heart, blood red!

And I saw in a vision how far and fleet
That fatal bullet went speeding forth,
Till it reached a town in the distant North,
Till it reached a house in a sunny street,
Till it reached a heart that ceased to beat
Without a murmur, without a cry;
And a bell was tolled in that far-off town,
For one who had passed from cross to crown,
And the neighbors wondered that she should die.

The Wound-Dresser

1

An old man bending I come among new faces,
Years looking backward resuming in answer to
  children,
Come tell us old man, as from young men and
  maidens that love me,
(Arous'd and angry, I'd thought to beat the alarum,
  and urge relentless war,
But soon my fingers fail'd me, my face droop'd and
  I resign'd myself,
To sit by the wounded and soothe them, or silently
  watch the dead;)
Years hence of these scenes, of these furious
  passions, these chances,
Of unsurpass'd heroes, (was one side so brave? the
  other was equally brave;)
Now be witness again, paint the mightiest armies
  of earth,
Of those armies so rapid so wondrous what saw
  you to tell us?
What stays with you latest and deepest? of curious
  panics,
Of hard-fought engagements or sieges tremendous
  what deepest remains?

2

O maidens and young men I love and that love me,
What you ask of my days those the strangest and
  sudden your talking recalls,
Soldier alert I arrive after a long march cover'd
  with sweat and dust,
In the nick of time I come, plunge in the fight,
  loudly shout in the rush of successful charge,
Enter the captur'd works—yet lo, like a swift-
  running river they fade,
Pass and are gone they fade—I dwell not on
  soldiers' perils or soldiers' joys,
(Both I remember well—many of the hardships,
  few the joys, yet I was content.)

But in silence, in dreams' projections,
While the world of gain and appearance and mirth
  goes on,
So soon what is over forgotten, and waves wash
  the imprints off the sand,
With hinged knees returning I enter the doors,
  (while for you up there,
Whoever you are, follow without noise and be of
  strong heart.)

continues

Bearing the bandages, water and sponge,
Straight and swift to my wounded I go,
Where they lie on the ground after the battle brought in,
Where their priceless blood reddens the grass the ground,
Or to the rows of the hospital tent, or under the roof'd hospital,
To the long rows of cots up and down each side I return,
To each and all one after another I draw near, not one do I miss,
An attendant follows holding a tray, he carries a refuse pail,
Soon to be fill'd with clotted rags and blood, emptied, and fill'd again.

I onward go, I stop,
With hinged knees and steady hand to dress wounds,
I am firm with each, the pangs are sharp yet unavoidable,
One turns to me his appealing eyes—poor boy! I never knew you,
Yet I think I could not refuse this moment to die for you, if that would save you.

3

On, on I go, (open doors of time! open hospital doors!)
The crush'd head I dress, (poor crazed hand tear not the bandage away,)
The neck of the cavalry-man with the bullet through and through I examine,
Hard the breathing rattles, quite glazed already the eye, yet life struggles hard,
(Come sweet death! be persuaded O beautiful death!
In mercy come quickly.)

From the stump of the arm, the amputated hand,
I undo the clotted lint, remove the slough, wash off the matter and blood,
Back on his pillow the soldier bends with curv'd neck and side falling head,
His eyes are closed, his face is pale, he dares not look on the bloody stump,
And has not yet look'd on it.

I dress a wound in the side, deep, deep,
But a day or two more, for see the frame all wasted and sinking,
And the yellow-blue countenance see.

continues

I dress the perforated shoulder, the foot with the bullet-wound,
Cleanse the one with a gnawing and putrid gangrene, so sickening, so offensive,
While the attendant stands behind aside me holding the tray and pail.

I am faithful, I do not give out,
The fractur'd thigh, the knee, the wound in the abdomen,
These and more I dress with impassive hand, (yet deep in my breast a fire, a burning flame.)

4

Thus in silence in dreams' projections,
Returning, resuming, I thread my way through the hospitals,
The hurt and wounded I pacify with soothing hand,
I sit by the restless all the dark night, some are so young,
Some suffer so much, I recall the experience sweet and sad,
(Many a soldier's loving arms about this neck have cross'd and rested,
Many a soldier's kiss dwells on these bearded lips.)

The Battle-Cry of Freedom

Yes, we'll rally round the flag, boys, we'll rally
 once again,
 Shouting the battle cry of Freedom;
We will rally from the hillside, we'll gather from
 the plain,
 Shouting the battle cry of Freedom.

Refrain:

The Union forever, Hurrah! boys, Hurrah!
Down with the traitor, up with the stars;
While we rally round the flag, boys, rally
 once again,
Shouting the battle cry of Freedom.

We are springing to the call of our brothers gone
 before,
 Shouting the battle cry of Freedom;
And we'll fill the vacant ranks with a million free
 men more,
 Shouting the battle cry of Freedom.

We will welcome to our numbers the loyal, true,
 and brave,
 Shouting the battle cry of Freedom;

stanza continues

GEORGE FREDERICK ROOT (1820–1895)

And although they may be poor, not a man shall be
a slave,
Shouting the battle cry of Freedom.

So we're springing to the call from the East and
from the West,
Shouting the battle cry of Freedom;
And we'll prove a loyal crew for the land we love
the best,
Shouting the battle cry of Freedom.

All Quiet Along the Potomac Tonight

"All quiet along the Potomac to-night!"
  Except here and there a stray picket
Is shot, as he walks on his beat, to and fro,
  By a rifleman hid in the thicket.

'Tis nothing! a private or two now and then
  Will not count in the news of a battle;
Not an officer lost! only one of the men
  Moaning out, all alone, the death-rattle.

All quiet along the Potomac to-night!
  Where soldiers lie peacefully dreaming;
And their tents in the rays of the clear autumn
    moon,
  And the light of their camp-fires are gleaming.

A tremulous sigh, as a gentle night-wind
  Through the forest leaves slowly is creeping;
While the stars up above, with their glittering eyes,
  Keep guard o'er the army while sleeping.

There's only the sound of the lone sentry's tread,
  As he tramps from the rock to the fountain,

stanza continues

And he thinks of the two on the low trundle bed,
Far away, in the cot on the mountain.

His musket falls slack, his face, dark and grim,
Grows gentle with memories tender,
As he mutters a prayer for the children asleep,
And their mother—"may heaven defend her!"

The moon seems to shine forth as brightly as then—
That night, when the love, yet unspoken,
Leaped up to his lips, and when low-murmured
vows
Were pledged to be ever unbroken.

Then drawing his sleeve roughly over his eyes,
He dashes off tears that are welling;
And gathers his gun closer up to his breast,
As if to keep down the heart's swelling.

He passes the fountain, the blasted pine-tree,
And his footstep is lagging and weary;
Yet onward he goes, through the broad belt of light,
Towards the shades of the forest so dreary.

Hark! was it the night wind that rustled the leaves?
Was it moonlight so wondrously flashing?

stanza continues

It looked like a rifle: "Ha! Mary, good-bye!"
  And his life-blood is ebbing and splashing.

"All quiet along the Potomac to-night!"
  No sound save the rush of the river;
While soft falls the dew on the face of the dead,
  And the picket's off duty forever!

The Battle Hymn of the Republic

Mine eyes have seen the glory of the coming of the
Lord;
He is trampling out the vintage where the grapes
of wrath are stored;
He hath loosed the fateful lightning of His terrible
swift sword;
His truth is marching on.

Glory! Glory! Hallelujah!
Glory! Glory! Hallelujah!
Glory! Glory! Hallelujah!
His truth is marching on.

I have seen Him in the watch fires of a hundred
circling camps
They have builded Him an altar in the evening
dews and damps;
I can read His righteous sentence by the dim and
flaring lamps;
His day is marching on.

Glory! Glory! Hallelujah!
Glory! Glory! Hallelujah!
Glory! Glory! Hallelujah!
His day is marching on.

JULIA WARD HOWE (1819–1910)

He has sounded forth the trumpet that shall never
call retreat;
He is sifting out the hearts of men before His
judgment seat;
Oh, be swift, my soul, to answer Him; be jubilant,
my feet;
Our God is marching on.

Glory! Glory! Hallelujah!
Glory! Glory! Hallelujah!
Glory! Glory! Hallelujah!
Our God is marching on.

In the beauty of the lilies Christ was born across
the sea,
With a glory in His bosom that transfigures you
and me;
As He died to make men holy, let us die to make
men free;
While God is marching on.

Glory! Glory! Hallelujah!
Glory! Glory! Hallelujah!
Glory! Glory! Hallelujah!
While God is marching on.

Shiloh: A Requiem

Skimming lightly, wheeling still,
  The swallows fly low
Over the field in clouded days,
  The forest-field of Shiloh—
Over the field where April rain
Solaced the parched ones stretched in pain
Through the pause of night
That followed the Sunday fight
  Around the church of Shiloh—
The church so lone, the log-built one,
That echoed to many a parting groan
    And natural prayer
  Of dying foemen mingled there—
Foemen at morn, but friends at eve—
  Fame or country least their care:
(What like a bullet can undeceive!)
  But now they lie low,
While over them the swallows skim,
  And all is hushed at Shiloh.

Barbara Frietchie

Up from the meadows rich with corn,
Clear in the cool September morn,

The clustered spires of Frederick stand
Green-walled by the hills of Maryland.

Round about them orchards sweep,
Apple and peach tree fruited deep,

Fair as the garden of the Lord
To the eyes of the famished Rebel horde,

On that pleasant morn of the early fall
When Lee marched over the mountain-wall;

Over the mountains winding down,
Horse and foot, into Frederick town.

Forty flags with their silver stars,
Forty flags with their crimson bars,

Flapped in the morning wind: the sun
Of noon looked down, and saw not one.

continues

Up rose old Barbara Frietchie then,
Bowed with her fourscore years and ten;

Bravest of all in Frederick town,
She took up the flag the men hauled down;

In her attic window the staff she set,
To show that one heart was loyal yet.

Up the street came the Rebel tread,
Stonewall Jackson riding ahead.

Under his slouched hat left and right
He glanced; the old flag met his sight.

"Halt!"—the dust-brown ranks stood fast.
"Fire!"—out blazed the rifle-blast.

It shivered the window, pane and sash;
It rent the banner with seam and gash.

Quick, as if fell, from the broken staff
Dame Barbara snatched the silken scarf.

She leaned far out on the window-sill,
And shook it forth with a royal will.

"Shoot, if you must, this old gray head,
But spare your country's flag," she said.

A shade of sadness, a blush of shame,
Over the face of the leader came;

The nobler nature within him stirred
To life at that woman's deed and word;

"Who touches a hair of yon gray head
Dies like a dog! March on!" he said.

All day long through Frederick street
Sounded the tread of marching feet:

All day long that free flag tossed
Over the heads of the Rebel host.

Ever its torn folds rose and fell
On the loyal winds that loved it well;

And through the hill-gaps sunset light
Shone over it with a warm good-night.

Barbara Frietchie's work is o'er,
And the Rebel rides on his raids no more.

continues

Honor to her! and let a tear
Fall, for her sake, on Stonewall's bier.

Over Barbara Frietchie's grave,
Flag of Freedom and Union, wave!

Peace and order and beauty draw
Round thy symbol of light and law;

And ever the stars above look down
On thy stars below in Frederick town!

President Lincoln's Proclamation of Freedom

It shall flash through the coming ages;
It shall light the distant years;
And eyes now dim with sorrow
Shall be clearer through their tears.

It shall flush the mountain ranges;
And the valleys shall grow bright;
It shall bathe the hills in radiance,
And crown their brows with light.

It shall flood with golden splendor
And the huts of Caroline,
And the sun-kissed brow of labor
With lustre new shall shine.

It shall gild the gloomy prison,
Darken'd by the nation's crime,
Where the dumb and patient millions
Wait the better coming time.

By the light that gilds their prison,
They shall seize its mould'ring key,

stanza continues

And the bolts and bars shall vibrate
  With the triumphs of the free.

Like the dim and ancient chaos,
  Shrinking from the dawn of light,
Oppression, grim and hoary,
  Shall cower at the sight.

And her spawn of lies and malice
  Shall grovel in the dust,
While joy shall thrill the bosoms
  Of the merciful and just.

Though the morning seemed to linger
  O'er the hill-tops far away,
Now the shadows bear the promise
  Of the quickly coming day.

Soon the mists and murky shadows
  Shall be fringed with crimson light,
And the glorious dawn of freedom
  Break refulgent on the sight.

The Black Regiment

Dark as the clouds of even,
Ranked in the western heaven,
Waiting the breath that lifts
All the dead mass, and drifts
Tempest and falling brand
Over a ruined land,—
So still and orderly,
Arm to arm, knee to knee,
Waiting the great event,
Stands the black regiment.

Down the long dusky line
Teeth gleam and eyeballs shine;
And the bright bayonet,
Bristling and firmly set,
Flashed with a purpose grand,
Long ere the sharp command
Of the fierce rolling drum
Told them their time had come,
Told them what work was sent
For the black regiment.

"Now," the flag-sergeant cried,
"Though death and hell betide,

stanza continues

Let the whole nation see
If we are fit to be
Free in this land; or bound
Down, like the whining hound,—
Bound with red stripes of pain
In our old chains again!"
Oh, what a shout there went
From the black regiment!

"Charge!" Trump and drum awoke;
Onward the bondmen broke;
Bayonet and saber-stroke
Vainly opposed their rush.
Through the wild battle's crush,
With but one thought aflush,
Driving their lords like chaff,
In the guns' mouths they laugh;
Or at the slippery brands,
Leaping with open hands,
Down they tear man and horse,
Down in their awful course;
Trampling with bloody heel
Over the crashing steel,
All their eyes forward bent,
Rushed the black regiment.

"Freedom!" their battle-cry,—
"Freedom! or leave to die!"
Ah! and they meant the word,
Not as with us 'tis heard,
Not a mere party shout:
They gave their spirits out;
Trusted the end to God,
And on the gory sod
Rolled in triumphant blood.
Glad to strike one free blow,
Whether for weal or woe;
Glad to breathe one free breath,
Though on the lips of death;
Praying,—alas! in vain!—
That they might fall again,
So they could once more see
That burst to liberty!
This was what "freedom" lent
To the black regiment

Hundreds on hundreds fell;
But they are resting well;
Scourges and shackles strong
Never shall do them wrong.
Oh, to the living few,
Soldiers, be just and true!

stanza continues

Hail them as comrades tried;
Fight with them side by side;
Never, in field or tent,
Scorn the black regiment!

Negro Soldier's Civil War Chant

Ole Abe (God bless 'is ole soul!)
Got a plenty good victuals, an' a plenty good clo'es.
Got powder, an' shot, an' lead,
To bust in Adam's liddle Confed'
In dese hard times.

Oh, once dere wus union, an' den dere wus peace;
De slave, in de cornfield, bare up to his knees.
But de Rebel's in gray, an' Sesesh's in de way,
An' de slave'll be free
In dese hard times.

ANONYMOUS (19TH CENTURY)

The Unsung Heroes

A song for the unsung heroes who rose in the
  country's need,
When the life of the land was threatened by the
  slaver's cruel greed,
For the men who came from the cornfield, who
  came from the plough and the flail,
Who rallied round when they heard the sound of
  the mighty man of the rail.

They laid them down in the valleys, they laid them
  down in the wood,
And the world looked on at the work they did, and
  whispered, "It is good."
They fought their way on the hillside, they fought
  their way in the glen,
And God looked down on their sinews brown, and
  said, "I have made them men."

They went to the blue lines gladly, and the blue
  lines took them in,
And the men who saw their muskets' fire thought
  not of their dusky skin.

stanza continues

The gray lines rose and melted beneath their
scathing showers,
And they said, " 'Tis true, they have force to do,
these old slave boys of ours."

Ah, Wagner saw their glory, and Pillow knew their
blood,
That poured on a nation's altar, a sacrificial flood.
Port Hudson heard their war-cry that smote its
smoke-filled air,
And the old free fires of their savage sires again
were kindled there.

They laid them down where the rivers, the
greening valleys gem.
And the song of the thund'rous cannon was their
sole requiem,
And the great smoke wreath that mingled its hue
with the dusky cloud,
Was the flag that furled o'er a saddened world,
and the sheet that made their shroud.

Oh, Mighty God of the Battles Who held them in
Thy hand,
Who gave them strength through the whole day's
length, to fight for their native land,

stanza continues

They are lying dead on the hillsides, they are lying
dead on the plain,
And we have not fire to smite the lyre and sing
them one brief strain.

Give, Thou, some seer the power to sing them in
their might,
The men who feared the master's whip, but did not
fear the fight;
That he may tell of their virtues as minstrels did
of old,
Till the pride of face and the hate of race grow
obsolete and cold.

A song for the unsung heroes who stood the awful
test,
When the humblest host that the land could boast
went forth to meet the best;
A song for the unsung heroes who fell on the
bloody sod,
Who fought their way from night to day and
struggled up to God.

John Burns of Gettysburg

Have you heard the story that gossips tell
Of Burns of Gettysburg? No? Ah, well:
Brief is the glory that hero earns,
Briefer the story of poor John Burns:
He was the fellow who won renown, —
The only man who didn't back down
When the rebels rode through his native town;
But held his own in the fight next day,
When all his townsfolk ran away.
That was in July, sixty-three, —
The very day that General Lee,
Flower of Southern chivalry,
Baffled and beaten, backward reeled
From a stubborn Meade and a barren field.

I might tell how, but the day before,
John Burns stood at his cottage door,
Looking down the village street,
Where, in the shade of his peaceful vine,
He heard the low of his gathered kine,
And felt their breath with incense sweet;
Or I might say, when the sunset burned
The old farm gable, he thought it turned

stanza continues

BRET HARTE (1836–1902)

The milk that fell like a babbling flood
Into the milk-pail, red as blood!
Or how he fancied the hum of bees
Were bullets buzzing among the trees.
But all such fanciful thoughts as these
Were strange to a practical man like Burns,
Who minded only his own concerns,
Troubled no more by fancies fine
Than one of his calm-eyed, long-tailed kine,—
Quite old-fashioned and matter-of-fact,
Slow to argue, but quick to act.
That was the reason, as some folks say,
He fought so well on that terrible day.

And it was terrible. On the right
Raged for hours the heady fight,
Thundered the battery's double bass,—
Difficult music for men to face;
While on the left—where now the graves
Undulate like the living waves
That all that day unceasing swept
Up to the pits the rebels kept—
Round-shot ploughed the upland glades,
Sown with bullets, reaped with blades;
Shattered fences here and there
Tossed their splinters in the air;
The very trees were stripped and bare;

stanza continues

The barns that once held yellow grain
Were heaped with harvests of the slain;
The cattle bellowed on the plain,
The turkeys screamed with might and main,
The brooding barn-fowl left their rest
With strange shells bursting in each nest.

Just where the tide of battle turns,
Erect and lonely, stood old John Burns.
How do you think the man was dressed?
He wore an ancient long buff vest,
Yellow as saffron,—but his best;
And, buttoned over his manly breast,
Was a bright blue coat, with a rolling collar,
And large gilt buttons,—size of a dollar,—
With tails that the country-folk called "swaller."
He wore a broad-brimmed, bell-crowned hat,
White as the locks on which it sat.
Never had such a sight been seen.
For forty years on the village green,
Since old John Burns was a country beau,
And went to the "quiltings" long ago.

Close at his elbows all that day,
Veterans of the Peninsula,
Sunburnt and bearded, charged away;

stanza continues

And striplings, downy of lip and chin,—
Clerks that the Home-Guard mustered in,—
Glanced, as they passed, at the hat he wore,
Then at the rifle his right hand bore;
And hailed him, from out their youthful lore,
With scraps of a slangy repertoire:
"How are you, White Hat?" "Put her through!"
"Your head's level!" and "Bully for you!"
Called him "Daddy,"—begged he'd disclose
The name of the tailor who made his clothes,
And what was the value he set on those;
While Burns, unmindful of jeer or scoff,
Stood there picking the rebels off,—
With his long brown rifle, and bell-crowned hat,
And the swallow-tails they were laughing at.

'Twas but a moment, for that respect
Which clothes all courage their voices checked;
And something the wildest could understand
Spake in the old man's strong right hand,
And his corded throat, and the lurking frown
Of his eyebrows under his old bell-crown;
Until, as they gazed, there crept an awe
Through the ranks in whispers, and some men saw,
In the antique vestments and long white hair,
The Past of the Nation in battle there;

stanza continues

And some of the soldiers since declare
That the gleam of his old white hat afar,
Like the crested plume of the brave Navarre,
That day was their oriflamme of war.

So raged the battle. You know the rest:
How the rebels, beaten and backward pressed,
Broke at the final charge and ran.
At which John Burns—a practical man—
Shouldered his rifle, unbent his brows,
And then went back to his bees and cows.

That is the story of old John Burns;
This is the moral the reader learns:
In fighting the battle, the question's whether
You'll show a hat that's white, or a feather!

from Gettysburg Ode

I

After the eyes that looked, the lips that spake
Here, from the shadows of impending death,
Those words of solemn breath,
What voice may fitly break
The silence, doubly hallowed, left by him?
We can but bow the head, with eyes grown dim,
And, as a Nation's litany, repeat
The phrase his martyrdom hath made complete,
Noble as then, but now more sadly-sweet:
"Let us, the Living, rather dedicate
Ourselves to the unfinished work, which they
Thus far advanced so nobly on its way,
And save the perilled State!
Let us, upon this field where they, the brave,
Their last full measure of devotion gave,
Highly resolve they have not died in vain! —
That, under God, the Nation's later birth
Of freedom, and the people's gain
Of their own Sovereignty, shall never wane
And perish from the circle of the earth!"
From such a perfect text, shall Song aspire
To light her faded fire,

And into wandering music turn
Its virtue, simple, sorrowful, and stern?
His voice all elegies anticipated;
For, whatsoe'er the strain,
We hear that one refrain:
"We consecrate ourselves to them, the Consecrated!"

The Master

A flying word from here and there
Had sown the name at which we sneered,
But soon the name was everywhere,
To be reviled and then revered:
A presence to be loved and feared,
We cannot hide it, or deny
That we, the gentlemen who jeered,
May be forgotten by and by.

He came when days were perilous
And hearts of men were sore beguiled;
And having made his note of us,
He pondered and was reconciled.
Was ever master yet so mild
As he, and so untamable?
We doubted, even when he smiled,
Not knowing what he knew so well.

He knew that undeceiving fate
Would shame us whom he served unsought;
He knew that he must wince and wait—
The jest of those for whom he fought;
He knew devoutly what he thought

stanza continues

Of us and of our ridicule;
He knew that we must all be taught
Like little children in a school.

We gave a glamour to the task
That he encountered and saw through,
But little of us did he ask,
And little did we ever do.
And what appears if we review
The season when we railed and chaffed?
It is the face of one who knew
That we were learning while we laughed.

The face that in our vision feels
Again the venom that we flung,
Transfigured to the world reveals
The vigilance to which we clung.
Shrewd, hallowed, harassed, and among
The mysteries that are untold,
The face we see was never young
Nor could it wholly have been old.

For he, to whom we had applied
Our shopman's test of age and worth,
Was elemental when he died,
As he was ancient at his birth:

stanza continues

The saddest among kings of earth,
Bowed with a galling crown, this man
Met rancor with a cryptic mirth,
Laconic—and Olympian.

The love, the grandeur, and the fame
Are bounded by the world alone;
The calm, the smouldering, and the flame
Of awful patience were his own:
With him they are forever flown
Past all our found self-shadowings,
Wherewith we cumber the Unknown
As with inept, Icarian wings.

For we were not as other men:
'Twas ours to soar and his to see;
But we are coming down again,
And we shall come down pleasantly;
Nor shall we longer disagree
On what it is to be sublime,
But flourish in our perigee
And have one Titan at a time.

The Martyr

Good Friday was the day
  Of the prodigy and crime,
When they killed him in his pity,
  When they killed him in his prime
Of clemency and calm—
    When with yearning he was filled
    To redeem the evil-willed,
And, though conqueror, be kind;
  But they killed him in his kindness,
  In their madness and their blindness,
And they killed him from behind.

    There is sobbing of the strong,
      And a pall upon the land;
    But the People in their weeping
        Bare the iron hand:
    Beware the People weeping
      When they bare the iron hand.

He lieth in his blood—
  The father in his face;
They have killed him, the Forgiver—
  The Avenger takes his place,

stanza continues

The Avenger wisely stern,
Who in righteousness shall do
What the heavens call him to,
And the parricides remand;
For they killed him in his kindness,
In their madness and their blindness,
And his blood is on their hand.

There is sobbing of the strong,
And a pall upon the land;
But the People in their weeping
Bare the iron hand:
Beware the People weeping
When they bare the iron hand.

O Captain! My Captain!

O Captain! my Captain! our fearful trip is done,
The ship has weather'd every rack, the prize we
  sought is won,
The port is near, the bells I hear, the people all
  exulting,
While follow eyes the steady keel, the vessel grim
  and daring;
    But O heart! heart! heart!
      O the bleeding drops of red,
        Where on the deck my Captain lies,
          Fallen cold and dead.

O Captain! my Captain! rise up and hear the bells;
Rise up—for you the flag is flung—for you the
  bugle trills,
For you bouquets and ribbon'd wreaths—for you
  the shores a-crowding,
For you they call, the swaying mass, their eager
  faces turning;
    Here Captain! dear father!
      The arm beneath your head!
        It is some dream that on the deck,
          You've fallen cold and dead.

continues

My captain does not answer, his lips are pale
  and still,
My father does not feel my arm, he has no pulse
  nor will,
The ship is anchor'd safe and sound, its voyage
  closed and done,
From fearful trip the victor ship comes in with
  object won:
    Exult O shores, and ring O bells!
      But I with mournful tread,
        Walk the deck my Captain lies,
          Fallen cold and dead.

When Johnny Comes Marching Home

When Johnny comes marching home again,
  Hurrah! hurrah!
We'll give him a hearty welcome then,
  Hurrah! hurrah!
The men will cheer, the boys will shout,
The ladies, they will all turn out,
  And we'll all feel gay,
When Johnny comes marching home.

The old church-bell will peal with joy,
  Hurrah! hurrah!
To welcome home our darling boy,
  Hurrah! hurrah!
The village lads and lasses say,
With roses they will strew the way;
  And we'll all feel gay,
When Johnny comes marching home.

Get ready for the jubilee,
  Hurrah! hurrah!
We'll give the hero three times three,
  Hurrah, hurrah!

stanza continues

The laurel-wreath is ready now
To place upon his loyal brow,
  And we'll all feel gay,
When Johnny comes marching home.

Let love and friendship on that day,
  Hurrah! hurrah!
Their choicest treasures then display,
  Hurrah! hurrah!
And let each one perform some part,
To fill with joy the warrior's heart;
  And we'll all feel gay,
When Johnny comes marching home.

The Blue and the Gray

By the flow of the inland river,
  Whence the fleets of iron have fled,
Where the blades of the grave-grass quiver,
  Asleep are the ranks of the dead:
    Under the sod and the dew,
      Waiting the Judgment Day:
    Under the one, the Blue,
      Under the other, the Gray.

These in the robings of glory,
  Those in the gloom of defeat,
All with the battle-blood gory,
  In the dusk of eternity meet:
    Under the sod and the dew,
      Waiting the Judgment Day:
    Under the laurel, the Blue,
      Under the willow, the Gray.

From the silence of sorrowful hours
  The desolate mourners go,
Lovingly laden with flowers
  Alike for the friend and the foe:
    Under the sod and the dew,
      Waiting the Judgment Day:

stanza continues

Under the roses, the Blue
Under the lilies, the Gray.

So with an equal splendor,
The morning sunrays fall,
With a touch impartially tender,
On the blossoms blooming for all:
Under the sod and the dew,
Waiting the Judgment Day:
Broidered with gold, the Blue,
Mellowed with gold, the Gray.

So, when the summer calleth,
On forest and field of grain,
With an equal murmur falleth
The cooling drip of the rain;
Under the sod and the dew,
Waiting the Judgment Day:
Wet with the rain, the Blue,
Wet with the rain, the Gray.

Sadly, but not with upbraiding,
The generous deed was done,
In the storm of the years that are fading
No braver battle was won:
Under the sod and the dew,

stanza continues

Waiting the Judgment Day:
Under the blossoms, the Blue,
Under the garlands, the Gray.

No more shall the war-cry sever,
Or the winding rivers be red;
They banish our anger forever
When they laurel the graves of our dead!
Under the sod and the dew,
Waiting the Judgment Day:
Love and tears for the Blue,
Tears and love for the Gray.

FRANCIS MILES FINCH (1827–1907)

Robert E. Lee

A gallant foeman in the fight,
  A brother when the fight was o'er,
The hand that led the host with might
  The blessed torch of learning bore.

No shriek of shells nor roll of drums,
  No challenge fierce, resounding far,
When reconciling Wisdom comes
  To heal the cruel wounds of war.

Thought may the minds of men divide,
  Love makes the heart of nations one,
And so, the soldier grave beside,
  We honor thee, Virginia's son.

JULIA WARD HOWE (1819–1910)

An Address by an Ex-Confederate Soldier to the Grand Army of the Republic

I

I was a rebel, if you please,
  A reckless fighter to the last,
Nor do I fall upon my knees
  And ask forgiveness for the past.

A traitor? *I* a traitor? No!
  I was a patriot to the core;
The South was mine, I loved her so,
  I gave her all,—I could no more.

You scowl at me. And was it wrong
  To wear the gray my father wore?
Could I slink back, though young and strong,
  From foes before my mother's door?

My mother's kiss was hot with fight,
  My father's frenzy filled his son,
Through reeking day and sodden night
  My sister's courage urged me on.

continues

And I, a missile steeped in hate,
  Hurled forward like a cannon-ball
By the resistless hand of fate,
  Rushed wildly, madly through it all.

I stemmed the level flames of hell,
  O'er bayonet bars of death I broke,
I was so near when Cleburne fell,
  I heard the muffled bullet stroke!

But all in vain. In dull despair
  I saw the storm of conflict die;
Low lay the Southern banner fair,
  And yonder flag was waving high.

God, what a triumph had the foe!
  Laurels, arches, trumpet-blare;
All around the earth their songs did go,
  Thundering through heaven their shouts
    did tear.

My mother, gray and bent with years,
  Hoarding love's withered aftermath,
Her sweet eyes burnt too dry for tears,
  Sat in the dust of Sherman's path.

My father, broken, helpless, poor,
  A gloomy, nerveless giant stood,
Too strong to cower and endure,
  Too weak to fight for masterhood.

My boyhood's home, a blackened heap
  Where lizards crawled and briers grew,
Had felt the fire of vengeance creep,
  The crashing round-shot hurtle through.

I had no country, all was lost,
  I closed my eyes and longed to die,
While past me stalked the awful ghost
  Of mangled, murdered Liberty.

The scars upon my body burned,
  I felt a heel upon my throat,
A heel that ground and grinding turned
  With each triumphal trumpet note.

"Grind on!" I cried, "nor doubt that I,
  (If all your necks were one and low
As mine is now) delightedly
  Would cut it by a single blow!"

continues

II

That was dark night; but day is here,
  The crowning victory is won;
Hark, how the sixty millions cheer,
  With Freedom's flag across the sun!

I a traitor! Who are *you*
  That dare to breathe that word to me?
You never wore the Union blue,
  No wounds attest *your* loyalty!

I do detest the sutler's clerk,
  Who skulked and dodged till peace had come,
Then found it most congenial work
  To beat the politician's drum.

I clasp the hand that made my scars,
  I cheer the flag my foemen bore,
I shout for joy to see the stars
  All on our common shield once more.

I do not cringe before you now,
  Or lay my face upon the ground;
I am a man, of men a peer,
  And not a cowering, cudgeled hound!

I stand and say that you were right,
  I greet you with uncovered head,
Remembering many a thundering fight,
  Where whistling death between us sped.

Remembering the boys in gray,
  With thoughts too deep and fine for words,
I lift this cup of love to-day
  To drink what only love affords.

Soldiers in blue, a health to you!
  Long life and vigor oft renewed,
While on your hearts, like honey-dew,
  Falls our great country's gratitude.

Lines

Sleep sweetly in your humble graves,
  Sleep martyrs of a fallen cause! —
Though yet no marble column craves
  The pilgrim here to pause.

In seeds of laurels in the earth,
  The garlands of your fame are sown;
And, somewhere, waiting for its birth,
  The shaft is in the stone.

Meanwhile, your sisters for the years
  Which hold in trust your storied tombs,
Bring all they now can give you — tears,
  And these memorial blooms.

Small tributes, but your shades will smile
  As proudly on those wreaths to-day,
As when some cannon-moulded pile
  Shall overlook this Bay.

Stoop angels hither from the skies!
  There is no holier spot of ground,
Than where defeated valor lies
  By mourning beauty crowned.

Memorial Day

The finest tribute we can pay
Unto our hero dead to-day,
Is not a rose wreath, white and red,
In memory of the blood they shed;
It is to stand beside each mound,
Each couch of consecrated ground,
And pledge ourselves as warriors true
Unto the work they died to do.

Into God's valleys where they lie
At rest, beneath the open sky,
Triumphant now, o'er every foe,
As living tributes let us go.
No wreath of rose or immortelles
Or spoken word or tolling bells
Will do to-day, unless we give
Our pledge that liberty shall live.

Our hearts must be the roses red
We place above our hero dead;
To-day beside their graves we must
Renew allegiance to their trust;

stanza continues

EDGAR A. GUEST (1881–1959)

Must bare our heads and humbly say
We hold the Flag as dear as they,
And stand, as once they stood, to die
To keep the Stars and Stripes on high.

The finest tribute we can pay
Unto our hero dead to-day
Is not of speech or roses red,
But living, throbbing hearts instead
That shall renew the pledge they sealed
With death upon the battlefield:
That freedom's flag shall bear no stain
And free men wear no tyrant's chain.

God Save the Flag!

Washed in the blood of the brave and the
    blooming,
  Snatched from the altars of insolent foes,
Burning with star-fires, but never consuming,
  Flash its broad ribbons of lily and rose.

Vainly the prophets of Baal would rend it,
  Vainly his worshippers pray for its fall;
Thousands have died for it, millions defend it,
  Emblem of justice and mercy to all:

Justice that reddens the sky with her terrors,
  Mercy that comes with her white-handed train,
Soothing all passions, redeeming all errors,
  Sheathing the sabre and breaking the chain.

Borne on the deluge of old usurpations,
  Drifted our Ark o'er the desolate seas,
Bearing the rainbow of hope to the nations,
  Torn from the storm-cloud and flung to the breeze!

God bless the Flag and its loyal defenders,
  While its broad folds o'er the battle-field wave,
Till the dim star-wreath rekindle its splendors,
  Washed from its stains in the blood of the brave!

OLIVER WENDELL HOLMES (1809–1894)

The Flag Goes By

Hats off!
Along the streets there comes
A blare of bugles, a ruffle of drums,
A flash of colour beneath the sky:
Hats off!
The flag is passing by!

Blue and crimson and white it shines
Over the steel-tipped, ordered lines.
Hats off!
The colours before us fly;
But more than the flag is passing by.

Sea-fights and land-fights, grim and great,
Fought to make and to save the State:
Weary marches and sinking ships;
Cheers of victory on dying lips;

Days of plenty and years of peace;
March of a strong land's swift increase;
Equal justice, right and law,
Stately honour and reverend awe;

Sign of a nation, great and strong
Toward her people from foreign wrong;
Pride and glory and honour, —all
Live in the colours to stand or fall.

Hats off!
Along the street there comes
A blare of bugles, a ruffle of drums;
And loyal hearts are beating high:
Hats off!
The flag is passing by!

America for Me

'Tis fine to see the Old World, and travel up and down
Among the famous palaces and cities of renown,
To admire the crumbly castles and the statues of the kings, —
But now I think I've had enough of antiquated things.

So it's home again, and home again, America for me!
My heart is turning home again, and there I long to be
In the land of youth and freedom beyond the ocean bars,
Where the air is full of sunlight and the flag is full of stars.

Oh, London is a man's town, there's power in the air;
And Paris is a woman's town, with flowers in her hair;
And it's sweet to dream in Venice, and it's great to study Rome,
But when it comes to living, there is no place like home.

 HENRY VAN DYKE (1852–1933)

I like the German fir-woods, in green battalions
  drilled;
I like the gardens of Versailles with flashing
  fountains filled;
But, oh, to take your hand, my dear, and ramble
  for a day
In the friendly western woodland where Nature
  has her way!

I know that Europe's wonderful, yet something
  seems to lack!
The Past is too much with her, and the people
  looking back.
But the glory of the Present is to make the Future
  free, —
We love our land for what she is and what she is
  to be.

Oh, it's home again, and home again, America
  for me!
I want a ship that's westward bound to plough
  the rolling sea,
To the blessed Land of Room Enough beyond
  the ocean bars,
Where the air is full of sunlight and the flag is
  full of stars.

I Hear America Singing

I hear America singing, the varied carols I hear,
Those of mechanics, each one singing his as it should be blithe and strong,
The carpenter singing his as he measures his plank or beam,
The mason singing his as he makes ready for work, or leaves off work,
The boatman singing what belongs to him in his boat, the deck-hand singing on the steamboat deck,
The shoemaker singing as he sits on his bench, the hatter singing as he stands,
The wood-cutters song, the ploughboy's on his way in the morning, or at noon intermission or at sundown,
The delicious singing of the mother, or of the young wife at work, or of the girl sewing or washing,
Each singing what belongs to him or her and to none else,
The day what belongs to the day—at night the party of young fellows, robust, friendly,
Singing with open mouths their strong melodious songs.

America

My country, 'tis of thee,
Sweet land of liberty,
  Of thee I sing;
Land where my fathers died,
Land of the pilgrims' pride,
From every mountain-side
  Let Freedom ring.

My native country, thee,
Land of the noble free,—
  Thy name I love;
I love thy rocks and rills,
Thy woods and templed hills;
My heart with rapture thrills
  Like that above.

Let music swell the breeze,
And ring from all the trees
  Sweet Freedom's song;
Let mortal tongues awake,
Let all that breathe partake,
Let rocks their silence break,—
  The sound prolong.

continues

SAMUEL FRANCIS SMITH (1808–1895)

Our fathers' God, to Thee,
Author of liberty,
   To Thee we sing;
Long may our land be bright
With Freedom's holy light;
Protect us by Thy might,
   Great God, our King.

Oh Mother of a Mighty Race

Oh mother of a mighty race,
Yet lovely in thy youthful grace!
The elder dames, thy haughty peers,
Admire and hate thy blooming years.
  With words of shame
And taunts of scorn they join thy name.

For on thy cheeks the glow is spread
That tints thy morning hills with red;
Thy step—the wild deer's rustling feet
Within thy woods are not more fleet;
  Thy hopeful eye
Is bright as thine own sunny sky.

Ay, let them rail—those haughty ones,
While safe thou dwellest with thy sons.
They do not know how loved thou art,
How many a fond and fearless heart
  Would rise to throw
Its life between thee and the foe.

They know not, in their hate and pride,
What virtues with thy children bide;

stanza continues

How true, how good, thy graceful maids
Make bright, like flowers, the valley-shades;
  What generous men
Spring, like thine oaks, by hill and glen;—

What cordial welcomes greet the guest
By thy lone rivers of the West;
How faith is kept, and truth revered,
And man is loved, and God is feared,
  In woodland homes,
And where the ocean border foams.

There's freedom at thy gates and rest
For Earth's down-trodden and oppressed,
A shelter for the hunted head,
For the starved laborer toil and bread.
  Power, at thy bounds.
Stops and calls back his baffled hounds.

Oh, fair young mother! on thy brow
Shall sit a nobler grace than now.
Deep in the brightness of the skies
The thronging years in glory rise,
  And, as they fleet,
Drop strength and riches at thy feet.

The Bartholdi Statue

The land, that, from the rule of kings,
In freeing us, itself made free,
Our Old World Sister, to us brings
Her sculptured Dream of Liberty:

Unlike the shapes of Egypt's sands
Uplifted by the toil-worn slave,
On Freedom's soil with freemen's hands
We rear the symbol free hands gave.

O France, the beautiful! to thee
Once more a debt of love we owe:
In peace beneath thy Colors Three,
We hail a later Rochambeau!

Rise, stately Symbol! holding forth
Thy light and hope to all who sit
In chains and darkness! Belt the earth
With watch-fires from thy torch up-lit!

Reveal the primal mandate still
Which Chaos heard and ceased to be,
Trace on mid-air th' Eternal Will
In signs of fire: "Let man be free!"

continues

Shine far, shine free, a guiding light
To Reason's ways and Virtue's aim,
A lightning-flash the wretch to smite
Who shields his license with thy name!

The New Colossus

Not like the brazen giant of Greek fame
With conquering limbs astride from land to land;
Here at our sea-washed, sunset gates shall stand
A mighty woman with a torch, whose flame
Is the imprisoned lightning, and her name
Mother of Exiles. From her beacon-hand
Glows world-wide welcome; her mild eyes
 command
The air-bridged harbor that twin cities frame,
"Keep, ancient lands, your storied pomp!" cries she
With silent lips, "Give me your tired, your poor,
Your huddled masses yearning to breathe free,
The wretched refuse of your teeming shore,
Send these, the homeless, tempest-tost to me,
I lift my lamp beside the golden door!"

EMMA LAZARUS (1849–1887)

When the Great Gray Ships Come In

To eastward ringing, to westward winging, o'er
  mapless miles of sea,
On winds and tides the gospel rides that the
  furthermost isles are free,
And the furthermost isles make answer, harbor,
  and height, and hill,
Breaker and beach cry each to each, " 'Tis the
  Mother who calls! Be still!"
Mother! new-found, belovèd, and strong to hold
  from harm,
Stretching to these across the seas the shield of her
  sovereign arm,
Who summoned the guns of her sailor sons, who
  bade her navies roam,
Who calls again to the leagues of main, and who
  tells them this time Home!

And the great gray ships are silent, and the weary
  watchers rest,
The black cloud dies in the August skies, and deep
  in the golden west
Invisible hands are limning a glory of crimson bars,
And far above is the wonder of a myriad wakened
  stars!

stanza continues

Peace! As the tidings silence the strenuous
cannonade,
Peace at last! is the bugle blast the length of the
long blockade,
And eyes of vigil weary are lit with the glad release,
From ship to ship and from lip to lip it is "Peace!
Thank God for peace."

Ah, in the sweet hereafter Columbia still shall
show
The sons of these who swept the seas how she
bade them rise and go,—
How, when the stirring summons smote on her
children's ear,
South and North at the call stood forth, and the
whole land answered, "Here!"
For the soul of the soldier's story and the heart of
the sailor's song
Are all of those who meet their foes as right should
meet with wrong,
Who fight their guns till the foeman runs, and
then, on the decks they trod,
Brave faces raise, and give the praise to the grace
of their country's God!

continues

Yes, it is good to battle, and good to be strong and
  free,
To carry the hearts of a people to the uttermost
  ends of the sea,
To see the day steal up the bay where the enemy
  lies in wait,
To run your ship to the harbor's lip and sink her
  across the strait:—
But better the golden evening when the ships
  round heads for home,
And the long gray miles slip swiftly past in a swirl
  of seething foam,
And the people wait at the haven's gate to greet the
  men who win!
Thank God for peace! Thank God for peace, when
  the great gray ships come in!

Mannahatta

I was asking for something specific and perfect for my city,
Whereupon lo! upsprang the aboriginal name.

Now I see what there is in a name, a word, liquid, sane, unruly, musical, self-sufficient,
I see that the word of my city is that word from of old,
Because I see that word nested in nests of water-bays, superb,
Rich, hemm'd thick all around with sailships and steamships, an island sixteen miles long, solid-founded,
Numberless crowded streets, high growths of iron, slender, strong, light, splendidly uprising toward clear skies,
Tides swift and ample, well-loved by me, toward sundown,
The flowing sea-currents, the little islands, larger adjoining islands, the heights, the villas,
The countless masts, the white shore-steamers, the lighters, the ferry-boats, the black sea-steamers well-model'd,

stanza continues

The down-town streets, the jobbers' houses of
  business, the houses of business of the ship-
  merchants and money-brokers, the river-streets,
Immigrants arriving, fifteen or twenty thousand in
  a week,
The carts hauling goods, the manly race of drivers
  of horses, the brown-faced sailors,
The summer air, the bright sun shining, and the
  sailing clouds aloft,
The winter snows, the sleigh-bells, the broken ice
  in the river, passing along up or down with the
  flood-tide or ebb-tide,
The mechanics of the city, the masters, well-
  form'd, beautiful-faced, looking you straight in
  the eyes,
Trottoirs throng'd, vehicles, Broadway, the women,
  the shops and shows,
A million people—manners free and superb—open
  voices—hospitality—the most courageous and
  friendly young men,
City of hurried and sparkling waters! city of spires
  and masts!
City nested in bays! my city!

Boston

My northern pines are good enough for me,
But there's a town my memory uprears —
A town that always like a friend appears,
And always in the sunrise by the sea.
And over it, somehow, there seems to be
A downward flash of something new and fierce,
That ever strives to clear, but never clears
The dimness of a charmed antiquity.

I know my Boston is a counterfeit, —
A frameless imitation, all bereft
Of living nearness, noise, and common speech;
But I am glad for every glimpse of it, —
And there it is, plain as a name that's left
In letters by warm hands I cannot reach.

Chicago

Hog Butcher for the World,
Tool Maker, Stacker of Wheat,
Player with Railroads and the Nation's Freight
Handler;
Stormy, husky, brawling,
City of the Big Shoulders:

They tell me you are wicked and I believe them,
for I have seen your painted women under the
gas lamps luring the farm boys.
And they tell me you are crooked and I answer:
Yes, it is true I have seen the gunman kill and go
free to kill again.
And they tell me you are brutal and my reply is:
On the faces of women and children I have seen
the marks of wanton hunger.
And having answered so I turn once more to those
who sneer at this my city, and I give them back
the sneer and say to them:
Come and show me another city with lifted head
singing so proud to be alive and coarse and
strong and cunning.

stanza continues

Flinging magnetic curses amid the toil of piling job
  on job, here is a tall bold slugger set vivid
  against the little soft cities;
Fierce as a dog with tongue lapping for action,
  cunning as a savage pitted against the
  wilderness,
    Bareheaded,
    Shoveling,
    Wrecking,
    Planning,
    Building, breaking, rebuilding,
Under the smoke, dust all over his mouth, laughing
  with white teeth,
Under the terrible burden of destiny laughing as a
  young man laughs,
Laughing even as an ignorant fighter laughs who
  has never lost a battle,
Bragging and laughing that under his wrist is the
  pulse, and under his ribs the heart of the people,
        Laughing!
Laughing the stormy, husky, brawling laughter of
  Youth, half-naked, sweating, proud to be Hog
  Butcher, Tool Maker, Stacker of Wheat, Player
  with Railroads and Freight Handler to the
  Nation.

The Western Home (Home on the Range)

Oh, give me a home where the buffalo roam,
Where the deer and the antelope play;
Where never is heard a discouraging word
And the sky is not clouded all day.

Oh, give me the gale of the Solomon vale
Where life streams with buoyancy flow,
On the banks of the Beaver, where seldom if ever
Any poisonous herbage doth grow.

Oh, give me the land where the bright diamond sand
Throws light from the glittering stream;
Where glideth along the graceful white swan,
Like a maid in her heavenly dreams.

I love these wild flowers in this bright land of our;
I love, too, the curlew's wild scream.
The bluffs of white rocks and antelope flocks
That graze on the hillsides so green.

How often at night, when the heavens are bright
By the light of the glittering stars,

stanza continues

Have I stood there amazed and asked as I gazed
If their beauty exceeds this of ours.

The air is so pure, the breezes so light,
The zephyrs so balmy at night,
I would not exchange my home here to range
Forever in azure so bright.

The New England Boy's Thanksgiving Day Song

Over the river, and through the wood,
To grandfather's house we go;
The horse knows the way,
To carry the sleigh,
Through the white and drifted snow.

Over the river, and through the wood—
Oh, how the wind does blow!
It stings the toes,
And bites the nose,
As over the ground we go.

Over the river, and through the wood,
To have a first-rate play.
Hear the bells ring,
"Ting-a-ling-ding!"
Hurrah for Thanksgiving Day!

Over the river and through the wood
Trot fast, my dapple-gray!
Spring over the ground
Like a hunting-hound!
For this is Thanksgiving Day.

Over the river and through the wood,
  And straight through the barn-yard gate.
    We seem to go
    Extremely slow,—
  It is so hard to wait!

Over the river and through the wood—
  Now grandmother's cap I spy!
    Hurrah for the fun!
    Is the pudding done?
  Hurrah for the pumpkin-pie!

The Old Camp-Fire

Now shift the blanket pad before your saddle back
you fling,
And draw your cinch up tighter till the sweat
drops from the ring:
We've a dozen miles to cover ere we reach the next
divide.
Our limbs are stiffer now than when we first set
out to ride,
And worse, the horses know it, and feel the leg-
grip tire,
Since in the days when, long ago, we sought the
old camp-fire.

Yes, twenty years! Lord! how we'd scent its incense
down the trail,
Through balm of bay and spice of spruce, when eye
and ear would fail,
And worn and faint from useless quest we crept,
like this, to rest,
Or, flushed with luck and youthful hope, we rode,
like this, abreast.
Ay! straighten up, old friend, and let the mustang
think he's nigher,
Through looser rein and stirrup strain, the
welcome old camp-fire.

BRET HARTE (1836–1902)

You know the shout that would ring out before us
  down the glade,
And start the blue jays like a flight of arrows
  through the shade,
And sift the thin pine needles down like slanting,
  shining rain,
And send the squirrels scampering back to their
  holes again,
Until we saw, blue-veiled and dim, or leaping
  like desire,
That flame of twenty years ago, which lit the old
  camp-fire.

And then that rest on Nature's breast, when talk
  had dropped, and slow
The night wind went from tree to tree with
  challenge soft and low!
We lay on lazy elbows propped, or stood to stir
  the flame,
Till up the soaring redwood's shaft our shadows
  danced and came,
As if to draw us with the sparks, high o'er its unseen
  spire,
To the five stars that kept their ward above the old
  camp-fire,—

continues

Those picket stars whose tranquil watch half
soothed, half shamed, our sleep.
What recked we then what beasts or men around
might lurk or creep?
We lay and heard with listless ears the far-off
panther's cry,
The near coyote's snarling snap, the grizzly's deep-
drawn sigh,
The brown bear's blundering human tread, the
gray wolves' yelping choir
Beyond the magic circle drawn around the old
camp-fire.

And then that morn! Was ever morn so filled with
all things new?
The light that fell through long brown aisles from
out the kinding blue,
The creak and yawn of stretching boughs, the jay-
bird's early call,
The rat-tat-tat of woodpecker that waked the
woodland hall,
The fainter stir of lower life in fern and brake
and brier,
Till flashing leaped the torch of Day from last
night's old camp-fire!

* * * *

Well, well! we'll see it once again; we should be
near it now;
It's scarce a mile to where the trail strikes off to
skirt the slough,
And then dip to Indian Spring, the wooded rise,
and—strange!
Yet here should stand the blasted pine that marked
our farther range;
And here—what's this? A ragged swale of ruts and
stumps and mire!
Sure this is not the sacred grove that hid the old
camp-fire!

Yet here's the "blaze" I cut myself, and there's the
stumbling ledge,
With quartz "outcrop" that lay atop, now leveled to
its edge,
And mounds of moss-grown stumps beside the
woodman's rotting chips,
And gashes in the hillside, that gape with dumb
red lips.
And yet above the shattered wreck and ruin,
curling higher—
Ah yes!—still lifts the smoke that marked the
welcome old camp-fire!

continues

Perhaps some friend of twenty years still lingers
there to raise
To weary hearts and tired eyes that beacon of
old days.
Perhaps—but stay; 't is gone! and yet once more it
lifts as though
To meet our tardy blundering steps, and seems to
move, and lo!
Whirls by us in a rush of sound,—the vanished
funeral pyre
Of hopes and fears that twenty years burned in the
old camp-fire!

For see, beyond the prospect spreads, with
chimney, spire, and roof,—
Two iron bands across the trail clank to our
mustang's hoof;
Above them leap two blackened threads from limb-
lopped tree to tree,
To where the whitewashed station speeds its
message to the sea.
Rein in! Rein in! the quest is o'er. The goal of our
desire
Is but the train whose track has lain across the old
camp-fire!

Casey Jones

Come all you rounders if you want to hear
The story of a brave engineer;
Casey Jones was the hogger's name,
On a big eight-wheeler, boys, he won his fame.
Caller called Casey at half-past four,
He kissed his wife at the station door,
Mounted to the cabin with orders in his hand,
And took his farewell trip to the promised land.

Casey Jones, he mounted to the cabin,
Casey Jones, with his orders in his hand!
Casey Jones, he mounted to the cabin,
Took his farewell trip into the promised land.

Put in your water and shovel in your coal,
Put your head out the window, watch the drivers
  roll,
I'll run her open till she leaves the rail,
'Cause we're eight hours late with the Western
  Mail!
He looked at his watch and his watch was slow,
Looked at the water and the water was low,
Turned to his fireboy and then he said,
"We'll get to 'Frisco, but we'll all be dead!"

continues

[CHORUS]

Casey pulled up old Reno Hill,
Tooted for the crossing with an awful shrill,
Snakes all knew by the engine's moans
That the hogger at the throttle was Casey Jones.
He pulled up short two miles from the place,
Number Four stared him right in the face,
Turned to his fireboy, said "You'd better jump,
'Cause there's two locomotives that're going to
bump!"

[CHORUS]

Casey said, just before he died,
"There's two more roads I'd like to ride."
Fireboy said, "What can they be?"
"The Rio Grande and the Old S.P."
Mrs. Jones sat on her bed a-sighing,
Got a telegram that Casey was dying,
Said, "Go to bed, children; hush your crying,
'Cause you've got another papa on the Salt Lake
Line."

Casey at the Bat

The outlook wasn't brilliant for the Mudville nine
that day;
The score stood four to two with but one inning
more to play.
And then when Cooney died at first, and Barrows
did the same,
A sickly silence fell upon the patrons of the game.

A straggling few got up to go in deep despair.
The rest
Clung to that hope which springs eternal in the
human breast;
They thought if only Casey could but get a whack
at that—
We'd put up even money now, with Casey at the bat.

But Flynn preceded Casey, as did also Jimmy
Blake,
And the former was a lulu, and the latter was
a cake;
So upon that stricken multitude grim melancholy
sat,
For there seemed but little chance of Casey's
getting to the bat.

continues

But Flynn let drive a single, to the wonderment
of all,
And Blake, the much despis-ed, tore the cover off
the ball;
And when the dust had lifted, and the men saw
what had occurred,
There was Johnnie safe at second and Flynn
a-hugging third.

Then from 5,000 throats and more there rose a
lusty yell;
It rumbled through the valley, it rattled in the dell;
It knocked upon the mountain and recoiled upon
the flat,
For Casey, mighty Casey, was advancing to
the bat.

There was ease in Casey's manner as he stepped
into his place;
There was pride in Casey's bearing and a smile on
Casey's face.
And when, responding to the cheers, he lightly
doffed his cap,
No stranger in the crowd could doubt 'twas Casey
at the bat.

Ten thousand eyes were on him as he rubbed his
hands with dirt;
Five thousand tongues applauded when he wiped
them on his shirt.
Then while the writhing pitcher ground the ball
into his hip,
Defiance gleamed in Casey's eye, a sneer curled
Casey's lip.

And now the leather-covered sphere came hurtling
through the air,
And Casey stood a-watching it in haughty
grandeur there.
Close by the sturdy batsman the ball unheeded
sped—
"That ain't my style," said Casey. "Strike one," the
umpire said.

From the benches, black with people, there went
up a muffled roar,
Like the beating of the storm-waves on a stern and
distant shore.
"Kill him! Kill the umpire!" shouted someone on
the stand;
And it's likely they'd have killed him had not Casey
raised his hand.

continues

With a smile of Christian charity great Casey's
visage shown;
He stilled the rising tumult; he bade the game go
on;
He signaled to the pitcher, and once more the
spheroid flew;
But Casey still ignored it, and the umpire said,
"Strike two."

"Fraud!" cried the maddened thousands, and echo
answered fraud;
But one scornful look from Casey and the audience
was awed.
They saw his face grow stern and cold, they saw
his muscles strain,
And they knew that Casey wouldn't let that ball go
by again.

The sneer is gone from Casey's lip, his teeth are
clinched in hate;
He pounds with cruel violence his bat upon the
plate.
And now the pitcher holds the ball, and now he
lets it go,
And now the air is shattered by the force of
Casey's blow.

Oh, somewhere in this favored land the sun is shining bright;
A band is playing somewhere, and somewhere hearts are light.
And somewhere men are laughing, and somewhere children shout;
But there is no joy in Mudville—mighty Casey has struck out.

Let America Be America Again

Let America be America again.
Let it be the dream it used to be.
Let it be the pioneer on the plain
Seeking a home where he himself is free.

(America never was America to me.)

Let America be the dream the dreamers dreamed—
Let it be that great strong land of love
Where never kings connive nor tyrants scheme
That any man be crushed by one above.

(It never was America to me.)

O, let my land be a land where Liberty
Is crowned with no false patriotic wreath,
But opportunity is real, and life is free,
Equality is in the air we breathe.

(There's never been equality for me,
Nor freedom in this "homeland of the free.")

Say, who are you that mumbles in the dark?
And who are you that draws your veil across the stars?

I am the poor white, fooled and pushed apart,
I am the Negro bearing slavery's scars.
I am the red man driven from the land,
I am the immigrant clutching the hope I seek—
And finding only the same old stupid plan
Of dog eat dog, of mighty crush the weak.

I am the young man, full of strength and hope,
Tangled in that ancient endless chain
Of profit, power, gain, of grab the land!
Of grab the gold! Of grab the ways of satisfying
  need!
Of work the men! Of take the pay!
Of owning everything for one's own greed!

I am the farmer, bondsman to the soil.
I am the worker sold to the machine.
I am the Negro, servant to you all.
I am the people, humble, hungry, mean—
Hungry yet today despite the dream.
Beaten yet today—O, Pioneers!
I am the man who never got ahead,
The poorest worker bartered through the years.

Yet I'm the one who dreamt our basic dream
In that Old World while still a serf of kings,
Who dreamt a dream so strong, so brave, so true,

stanza continues

That even yet its mighty daring sings
In every brick and stone, in every furrow turned
That's made America the land it has become.
O, I'm the man who sailed those early seas
In search of what I meant to be my home—
For I'm the one who left dark Ireland's shore,
And Poland's plain, and England's grassy lea,
And torn from Black Africa's strand I came
To build a "homeland of the free."

The free?

Who said the free? Not me?
Surely not me? The millions on relief today?
The millions shot down when we strike?
The millions who have nothing for our pay?
For all the dreams we've dreamed
And all the songs we've sung
And all the hopes we've held
And all the flags we've hung,
The millions who have nothing for our pay—
Except the dream that's almost dead today.

O, let America be America again—
The land that never has been yet—
And yet must be—the land where *every* man is free.

stanza continues

The land that's mine—the poor man's, Indian's,
Negro's, ME—
Who made America,
Whose sweat and blood, whose faith and pain,
Whose hand at the foundry, whose plow in
the rain,
Must bring back our mighty dream again.

Sure, call me any ugly name you choose—
The steel of freedom does not stain.
From those who live like leeches on the people's
lives,
We must take back our land again,
America!

O, yes,
I say it plain,
America never was America to me,
And yet I swear this oath—
America will be!

Out of the rack and ruin of our gangster death,
The rape and rot of graft, and stealth, and lies,
We, the people, must redeem
The land, the mines, the plants, the rivers.
The mountains and the endless plain—
All, all the stretch of these great green states—
And make America again!

The Congressional Library

The earth is a colored thing.
See the red clays, and the umbers and salt greys of
  the mountains;
See the clustered and wandering greens of plains
  and hillsides,
The leaf-greens, bush-greens, water-plant and
  snow-greens
Of gardens and forests.
See the reds of flowers—hibiscus, poppy,
  geranium;
The rose-red of little flowers—may-flowers,
  primroses;
The harlequin shades of sweet-peas, orchids,
  pansies;
The madders, saffrons, chromes, of still waters,
The silver and star-blues, the wine-blues of seas
  and oceans.
Observe the stars at nighttime, name the color of
  them;
Count and recount the hues of clouds at sunset and
  at dawn.
And the colors of the races of men—
What are they?
And what are we?

stanza continues

We, the people without a race,
Without a language;
Of all races, and of none;
Of all tongues, and one imposed;
Of all traditions and all pasts,
With no tradition and no past.
A patchwork and an altar-piece,
Vague as sea-mist,
Myriad as forest-trees,
Living into a present,
Building a future.
Our color is the vari-colored world.
No colors clash,
All clash and change,
And, in changing, new colors come and go and
  dominate and remain,
And no one shall say which remain,
Since those that have vanished return,
And those no man has seen take the light and are.

Where else in all America are we so symbolized
As in this hall?
White columns polished like glass,
A dome and a dome,
A balcony and a balcony,
Stairs and the balustrades to them,

stanza continues

Yellow marble and red slabs of it,
All mounting, spearing, flying into color.
Color round the dome and up to it,
Color curving, kite-flying, to the second dome,
Light, dropping, pitching down upon the color,
Arrow-falling upon the glass-bright pillars,
Mingled colors spinning into a shape of white
  pillars,
Fusing, cooling, into balanced shafts of shrill and
  interthronging light.
This is America,
This vast, confused beauty,
This staring, restless speed of loveliness,
Mighty, overwhelming, crude, of all forms,
Making grandeur out of profusion,
Afraid of no incongruities,
Sublime in its audacity,
Bizarre breaker of moulds,
Laughing with strength,
Charging down on the past,
Glorious and conquering,
Destroyer, builder,
Invincible pith and marrow of the world,
An old world remaking,
Whirling into the no-world of all-colored light.

But behind the vari-colored hall?
The entrails, the belly,
The blood-run veins, the heart and viscera,
What of these?
Only at night do they speak,
Only at night do the voices rouse themselves and speak.
There are words in the veins of this creature,
There are still notes singing in its breast:
Silent voices, whispering what it shall speak,
Frozen music beating upon its pulses.
These are the voices of the furious dead who never die,
Furious with love, and life, unquenchable,
Dictating their creeds across the vapors of time.
This is the music of the Trumpeters of the Almighty
Weeping for a lost estate,
Sounding to a new birth which is tomorrow.
Hark! This hurricane of music has no end,
The speech of these voices has neither end nor beginning;
They are inter-riven as the colors of the sky
Over the graveyards of ten thousand generations.

continues

When we are as Nineveh, our white columns
  thrown and scattered,
Our dome of colors striped with the crawling of
  insects,
Spotted with the thrust of damp clay—
Our words, our music, who will build a dome to
  hive them?
In whose belly shall we come to life?
A new life,
Beyond submergence and destruction,
The implacable life of silent words,
Of tumultuous stillness of never-ceasing music,
Lost to being that so it may triumph
And become the blood and heat and urge
Of that hidden distance which forever whips and
  harries the static present
Of mankind.

On the Pulse of Morning

A Rock, A River, A Tree
Hosts to species long since departed,
Marked the mastodon,
The dinosaur, who left dried tokens
Of their sojourn here
On our planet floor,
Any broad alarm of their hastening doom
Is lost in the gloom of dust and ages.

But today, the Rock cries out to us, clearly, forcefully,
Come, you may stand upon my
Back and face your distant destiny,
But seek no haven in my shadow,
I will give you no hiding place down here.

You, created only a little lower than
The angels, have crouched too long in
The bruising darkness
Have lain too long
Facedown in ignorance,
Your mouths spilling words

Armed for slaughter.
The Rock cries out to us today,

stanza continues

You may stand upon me;
But do not hide your face.

Across the wall of the world,
A River sings a beautiful song. It says,
Come, rest here by my side.

Each of you, a bordered country,
Delicate and strangely made proud,
Yet thrusting perpetually under siege.
Your armed struggles for profit
Have left collars of waste upon
My shore, currents of debris upon my breast.
Yet today I call you to my riverside,
If you will study war no more.
Come, clad in peace,
And I will sing the songs
The Creator gave to me when I and the
Tree and the Rock were one.
Before cynicism was a bloody sear across your brow
And when you yet knew you still knew nothing.
The River sang and sings on.

There is a true yearning to respond to
The singing River and the wise Rock.

stanza continues

So say the Asian, the Hispanic, the Jew
The African, the Native American, the Sioux,
The Catholic, the Muslim, the French, the Greek,
The Irish, the Rabbi, the Priest, the Sheik,
The Gay, the Straight, the Preacher,
The privileged, the homeless, the Teacher.
They hear. They all hear
The speaking of the Tree.

They hear the first and last of every Tree
Speak to humankind today.
Come to me,
Here beside the River.
Plant yourself beside the River.

Each of you, descendant of some passed-
On traveler, has been paid for.
You, who gave me my first name, you,
Pawnee, Apache, Seneca, you
Cherokee Nation, who rested with me, then
Forced on bloody feet,
Left me to the employment of
Other seekers—desperate for gain,
Starving for gold.

You, the Turk, the Arab, the Swede,
The German, the Eskimo, the Scot,

stanza continues

The Italian, the Hungarian, the Pole,
You the Ashanti, the Yoruba, the Kru, bought
Sold, stolen, arriving on a nightmare
Praying for a dream.
Here, root yourselves beside me.
I am that Tree planted by the River,
Which will not be moved.
I, the Rock, I, the River, I, the Tree
I am yours—your passages have been paid.
Lift up your faces, you have a piercing need
For this bright morning dawning for you.
History, despite its wrenching pain,
Cannot be unlived, but if faced
With courage, need not be lived again.

Lift up your eyes
Upon this day breaking for you.
Give birth again
To the dream.

Women, children, men,
Take it into the palms of your hands,
Mold it into the shape of your most
Private need. Sculpt it into
The image of your most public self.
Lift up your hearts

stanza continues

Each new hour holds new chances
For a new beginning.
Do not be wedded forever
To fear, yoked eternally
To brutishness.

The horizon leans forward,
Offering you space
To place new steps of change
Here, on the pulse of this fine day
You may have the courage
To look up and out and upon me,
The Rock, the River, the Tree, your country.
No less to Midas than the mendicant.
No less to you now than the mastodon then.

Here on the pulse of this new day
You may have the grace to look up and out
And into your sister's eyes,
And into your brother's face,
Your country,
And say simply
Very simply
With hope—
Good morning.

America the Beautiful

O beautiful for spacious skies,
  For amber waves of grain,
For purple mountain majesties
  Above the fruited plain!
America! America!
  God shed His grace on thee
And crown thy good with brotherhood
  From sea to shining sea!

O beautiful for pilgrim feet,
  Whose stern, impassioned stress
A thoroughfare for freedom beat
  Across the wilderness!
America! America!
  God mend thine every flaw,
Confirm their soul in self-control,
  Thy liberty in law!

O beautiful for heroes proved
  In liberating strife,
Who more than self their country loved,
  And mercy more than life!
America! America!
  May God thy gold refine,
Till all success be nobleness
  And every gain divine!

KATHARINE LEE BATES (1859–1929)

O beautiful for patriot dream
  That sees beyond the years
Thine alabaster cities gleam
  Undimmed by human tears!
America! America!
  God shed His grace on thee,
And crown thy good with brotherhood
  From sea to shining sea!

This Land Is Your Land©

This land is your land, This land is my land,
From California to the New York island;
From the redwood forest to the Gulf Stream waters:
This land was made for you and me.

As I was walking that ribbon of highway,
I saw above me that endless skyway:
I saw below me that golden valley:
This land was made for you and me.

I've roamed and rambled and I followed my footsteps
To the sparkling sands of her diamond deserts;
And all around me a voice was sounding:
This land was made for you and me.

When the sun came shining, and I was strolling,
And the wheat fields waving and the dust clouds
rolling,
As the fog was lifting a voice was chanting:
This land was made for you and me.

As I went walking, I saw a sign there,
And on the sign it said "No Trespassing."
But on the other side it didn't say nothing,
That side was made for you and me.

In the shadow of the steeple I saw my people,
By the relief office I seen my people;
As they stood there hungry, I stood there asking
Is this land made for you and me?

Nobody living can ever stop me,
As I go walking that freedom highway;
Nobody living can ever make me turn back,
This land was made for you and me.

Index of Authors

Index of First Lines

Acknowledgments

"On the Pulse of Morning," by Maya Angelou. Copyright © 1993 by Maya Angelou. Reprinted by permission of The Helen Brann Agency, Inc.

"The Gift Outright," from THE POETRY OF ROBERT FROST edited by Edward Connery Lathem. Copyright © 1942 by Robert Frost, © 1970 by Lesley Frost Ballantine, © 1969 by Henry Holt and Company. Reprinted by permission of Henry Holt and Company, LLC.

"This Land Is Your Land," Words & Music by Woody Guthrie. TRO © Copyright 1956 (Renewed) 1958 (Renewed), 1970 and 1972. Ludlow Music, Inc., New York, NY. Used by permission.

"Let America Be America Again," by Langston Hughes. From THE COLLECTED POEMS OF LANGSTON HUGHES by Langston Hughes, copyright © 1994 by The Estate of Langston Hughes. Used by permission of Alfred A. Knopf, a division of Random House, Inc.